e Open
University

first level
disciplinary
course

Using **Mathematics**

BLOCK C
CONTINUOUS MODELS

Choosing a function
for a model

APTER
C3

Prepared by the course team

About this course

This course, MST121 *Using Mathematics*, and the courses MU120 *Open Mathematics* and MS221 *Exploring Mathematics* provide a flexible means of entry to university-level mathematics. Further details may be obtained from the address below.

MST121 uses the software program Mathcad (MathSoft, Inc.) and other software to investigate mathematical and statistical concepts and as a tool in problem solving. This software is provided as part of the course, and its use is covered in the associated Computer Book.

The Open University, Walton Hall, Milton Keynes, MK7 6AA.

First published 1997. Reprinted 1997

Edited, designed and typeset by the Open University using the Open University TEX System.

Printed in the United Kingdom by Caligraving Limited, Thetford, Norfolk.

ISBN 0 7492 7870 6

This text forms part of an Open University First Level Course. If you would like a copy of *Studying with The Open University*, please write to the Course Enquiries Data Service, PO Box 625, Dane Road, Milton Keynes, MK1 1TY. If you have not already enrolled on the Course and would like to buy this or other Open University material, please write to Open University Educational Enterprises Ltd, 12 Cofferidge Close, Stony Stratford, Milton Keynes, MK11 1BY, United Kingdom.

1.2

Contents

Study guide

This chapter is shorter than Chapters C1 and C2, and we would recommend you to schedule four study sessions for your work on it. The study pattern which we recommend is as follows.

Study session 1: Section 1.

Study session 2: Section 2.

Study session 3: Section 3.

Study session 4: Sections 4 and 5. You will need access to your computer for Section 5, and to the Mathcad files for Block C.

An alternative pattern would be to interleave the computing work with your study of the main text. In this case, Section 3 together with its computing work would probably be too long for one study session, and we would recommend the following alternative.

Alternative study session 1: Section 1.

Alternative study session 2: Section 2 and Subsection 5.1.

Alternative study session 3: Subsections 3.1–3.4 and 5.2.

Alternative study session 4: Subsections 3.5, 3.6; Section 4; Subsection 5.3.

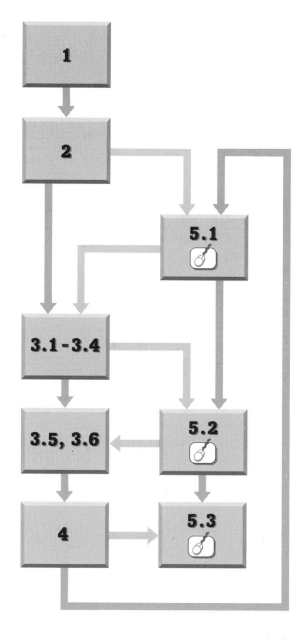

Introduction

You may have noticed how the two themes of (a) mathematical ideas and techniques and (b) the usefulness of mathematics in modelling have been running side by side in the course. This chapter continues this process, with regard to continuous rather than discrete models, and incorporates the ideas of differentiation and integration that you have encountered recently. The techniques of calculus are powerful and open the door to many modelling possibilities, so this chapter is intended to consolidate some modelling concepts. Let us start by reminding ourselves of the various steps of the modelling cycle, but state them in a slightly expanded form.

Step 1 **Specify the purpose** (of the model).

Step 2 **Create the** (mathematical) **model** (after making and stating relevant assumptions).

Step 3 **Do the** (resulting) **mathematics**.

Step 4 **Interpret the results**.

Step 5 **Evaluate the outcomes** (usually by comparing with reality and/or purpose).

Much of this chapter is concerned with Steps 2 and 3 of the cycle: *creating the mathematical model* and *doing the mathematics*. An important part of Step 2 is choosing an *appropriate* function based on the assumptions made also as part of this step. This choice will influence the kind of mathematical activity that is involved in Step 3.

So far in the course you have had little opportunity to think about what is appropriate, since the type of function to be used has been chosen for you. Indeed, the function to be used in the modelling may have been specified without any justification of why it is appropriate. Sometimes, however, you may be faced with making appropriate choices of function for yourself, so it is important to understand what might be appropriate in any given circumstance. A well-chosen function will be appropriate in two different ways. First, the function should be consistent with the purpose of the model, with known *data* or *theory* or *facts*, and with known or assumed *behaviour*. For example, if the purpose is to predict the future behaviour of something which is expected to increase with time, then the function chosen should be one in which the value of the dependent variable increases with time (which would be the independent variable in this case). Second, the initial choice of function should be as simple as allowed by the modelling context. The main reason for doing this is to avoid complication unless it is really necessary, bearing in mind that the modelling cycle is a cycle and so it is possible, and usual, to go round it more than once. Philosophically, an initial choice of a simple function is consistent with the fundamental belief that most phenomena may be modelled adequately by simple laws and theories. This has been a guiding principle behind scientific research since the Renaissance. It is fundamental to engineering practice always to try the simplest model that can be used in a given situation. So, for the first trip around the cycle, the appropriate function should be the simplest that is consistent with known facts, behaviours, theory or data. This might be a constant or a linear function. If the first choice turns out to be inadequate at the stage of the cycle where the result is interpreted or the outcome is evaluated (Step 5), then it is reasonable to try something more complicated; a quadratic function might be the second choice if the first choice were linear.

It is important to realise that sophistication is not necessarily a virtue in itself. The merits of complication depend upon the purpose for which the model is being formulated. A model of the weather that enables a decision on whether or not to take an umbrella to work on any particular day will be rather less sophisticated than that required to give an accurate prediction of the amount of rainfall in the vicinity of the workplace on that day.

In this chapter we shall look at various types of functions that have been introduced so far but in a different way, concentrating more on their graphical behaviour and their parameters. The basic structure of the chapter is to proceed from simpler to more complicated functions: constant and linear functions in Section 1; quadratic functions in Section 2; exponential, logarithmic and related functions in Section 3; oscillating functions in Section 4. Then in Section 5, you are asked to explore some of the functions and their graphical representations using Mathcad.

As mentioned earlier, appropriateness is determined by the extent to which the *behaviour* of the chosen function as the independent variable varies reflects the behaviour to be modelled. The behaviour of a function is determined by whether it is linear, non-linear or periodic, and on its range of validity. If it is non-linear, then there may be modelling significance not only in the behaviour of the function itself, but also in the behaviour of the derivative or derived function. Sometimes the behaviour of the derivative of the derivative or, indeed, that of the derivative of the derivative of the derivative, are significant; and so on. An important task of this chapter is to get you to think more and more in modelling terms about the forms and associated behaviours of functions. Also we shall take the opportunity of deriving some generalities from specific examples.

As part of your work on this block, you may well have been involved in learning new notation. Some of the learning file activities have encouraged you to explore ways of working on this, for example by reading the mathematics out loud. You may wish to continue this as you work through this chapter.

Using your Handbook effectively in this course may help you to improve your use of other reference documents now and in the future.

Also in this chapter you will be faced with a number of terms that you need to be familiar with and use. This provides you with the chance to review your use of the course Handbook in annotating terms, techniques, and so on. Annotating a handbook requires you to be clear and concise, skills which are also useful when creating your own summaries of what you have learned. In this chapter the main learning skills focus is on using a table to help create structured summaries. There is no Learning File sheet for this, as you will need to make judgements about the way you wish to lay out your own summary tables.

The other learning skills theme is directly related to the main theme of the chapter – that is, choosing an appropriate function for a model using the information you are given. This aspect, in fact, draws together much of the work you have been doing in this block.

1 Modelling with linear functions

1.1 Constant functions

There are two physical interpretations of constancy that are of interest here.

A very common form is *constancy with time*. Motion under gravity may be modelled as motion with constant acceleration. By definition, fixed-rate mortgages (increasingly popular in the late 1990s) offer a constant rate of interest over a specified period. In these examples, the constancy will be limited to a certain time interval. Motion under gravity will involve only the constant acceleration due to the earth's gravitational pull as long as the motion is close to the earth's surface. In any case the acceleration will only be from the time the object is released to the time it stops. Unfortunately, increases in base interest rates eventually feed into mortgage rates. So mortgage lenders are able to offer fixed rates only for a certain time. A mathematical statement of these limits is a statement of the *range of validity* of the constant function model.

Another type of constancy is *constancy in space*. Long stretches of Roman roads were built in a fixed direction. For at least part of their lengths, roads have constant width. In modelling the formation and movement of seismic waves in the earth's crust, it is convenient to assume that the layers from which the crust is formed have constant thickness with respect to the earth's surface. In these cases the assumption of constancy will be valid only within certain limits in space.

You may remember the motion of various joggers in Chapter C1, Section 1. One of the joggers, Tom, described as a steady jogger, was assumed to maintain a constant velocity along the street. This ignored any jerkiness in his motion over a 100 m length of street and during the 30 s it took him to travel the length of the street. Tom's speed worked out to be $\frac{10}{3}$ m s^{-1}.

So, if Tom's instantaneous speed is represented by v m s^{-1}, and time since he started along the street is denoted by t s, one way of writing down the model for Tom's jogging is

In this chapter, as in previous ones, symbols are used to represent numbers and the units are specified separately.

$$v = \frac{10}{3} \qquad (0 \leq t \leq 30).$$

Note that this is consistent with a constant speed during the 30 s of jogging. A graph of the variation (or non-variation!) of Tom's speed with time is the straight line parallel to the time axis as shown in Figure 1.1.

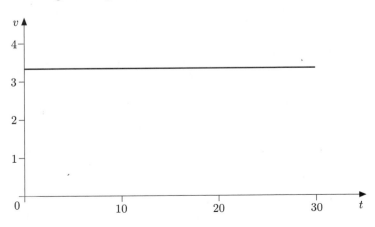

Figure 1.1

The assumption of constancy might be expressed in terms of the rate of change of a quantity rather than the quantity itself. <u>If a quantity is assumed constant, then</u> the implication is that <u>the rate of change of that quantity is zero.</u>

Acceleration and velocity have direction as well as magnitude. They are called *vector quantities*. Speed is the magnitude of velocity. A statement about velocity is always accompanied by an explicit or implicit direction as well as magnitude.

Since acceleration represents the rate of change of velocity (v) with time, and Tom's velocity is constant, his acceleration during this part of his jog is zero. The latter fact may be represented by

$$\frac{dv}{dt} = 0 \qquad (0 \leq t \leq 30).$$

Although this equation is also consistent with a constant velocity over 30 s, it does not contain as much information as the earlier one about v, since it implies *only* that Tom's velocity is constant and does not indicate what his velocity is. Integration of this relationship alone would lead to the conclusion that v is constant, but other information would be needed (for example, distance along the street or velocity at any particular time) to deduce the value of that constant.

On the other hand, suppose that we are more interested in Tom's *position* at any time than in his velocity. Using ideas from Chapter C2, Section 3, it is possible to note that velocity is itself rate of change of position, and to use the statement that v is constant to deduce something about the rate of change of position (s).

$$\frac{ds}{dt} = \frac{10}{3} \qquad (0 \leq t \leq 30).$$

Integration of this then results in

$$s = \frac{10}{3}t + c \qquad (0 \leq t \leq 30).$$

As long as we take Tom's location to be at $s = 0$ when $t = 0$, then $c = 0$. So

$$s = \frac{10}{3}t \qquad (0 \leq t \leq 30),$$

and the assumption of constant velocity results in Tom's position being a linear function of time. A graph of the variation of Tom's position with time is a straight line passing through $(0, 0)$ and $(30, 100)$ as in Figure 1.2. You may recall plotting this when studying Chapter C1.

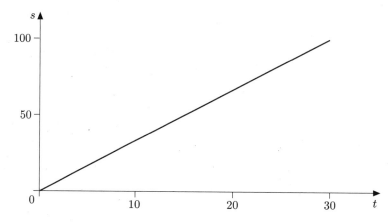

Figure 1.2

The assumption that one variable is constant may lead to a linear relationship between two other variables where a derivative is involved.

Note that zero acceleration may also be expressed in terms of position, as

$$\frac{d^2s}{dt^2} = 0 \qquad (0 \le t \le 30).$$

There is no particular reason for expressing Tom's motion in this way since he has zero acceleration, but a second-order differential equation of this type is more significant for non-zero acceleration, as will become clear in Activity 1.2.

Activity 1.1   A model for water flow

Suppose that a tap is turned on and that the rate of water running out of it, r litres per minute, is assumed to be constant at 3 litres per minute; assume also that it is turned off after 10 minutes.

r = 3 (0≤t≤ 10)

(a) Write down a mathematical statement of the model for the flow from the tap, including its range of validity. (Use t to denote the time in minutes since the tap was turned on.)

(b) Sketch a graph of the variation of r with t.

(c) Write down an expression for the gradient of the resulting curve and state its value.

r=3   dr = 0 (0≤t≤10)
dt

(d) Find an equation for the number, v, of litres of water that have run out of the tap after t minutes.

v = rt   (0≤t≤10)

(e) Calculate the volume of water that has run out of the tap three minutes before it is turned off.

v = 3×7 = 21ℓ

Comment

Solutions are given on page 65.

Activity 1.2   Motion under constant acceleration

v = 0 ms⁻¹
t=0   t=60s
a = 10 ms⁻²

An object is assumed to be moving in a given direction with a constant acceleration of $10\,\mathrm{m\,s^{-2}}$ during a one minute interval after it starts from rest. Denote acceleration in the given direction by $a\,\mathrm{m\,s^{-2}}$, velocity in the given direction by $v\,\mathrm{m\,s^{-1}}$, time by $t\,\mathrm{s}$, and write down:

a = 10

(a) an expression for acceleration including its range of validity;

dv = 10   (0≤t≤60)
dt

(b) an expression for rate of change of velocity;

(c) an expression for velocity in terms of time;

v = 10t

(d) an expression for distance travelled in the given direction from the starting position in terms of time;

(e) the type of function for distance travelled that has resulted from the initial assumption of constant acceleration.

Comment

Solutions are given on page 65.

Activity 1.3   Constant rate of change

Think about the implications of assuming that the rate of change of a quantity (rather than the quantity itself) is constant. For example, what does the assumption of constant acceleration mean about velocity? What does the assumption of constant velocity mean about position? What does the assumption of constant acceleration mean about position?

If the rate of change of a quantity is constant, the quantity itself varies linearly

9

Comment

Suggested solutions are given on page 65.

1.2 Linear functions

Activity 1.4   Recalling earlier models

Look back through Chapters A1, B2 and A4 to find examples of linear sequences and functions in modelling.

Comment

Suggested solutions are given on page 65.

The audio tape associated with Chapter A4 began by introducing linear functions of the form $y = mx + c$. Such functions give rise to straight-line graphs (see Figure 1.3). The coefficient m is the slope. If m is positive the graph of y against x slopes upwards. If m is negative the graph slopes downwards. The coefficient c gives the y-intercept (that is, the intercept on the y-axis). The quantities m and c are the **parameters** of the line. When modelling velocity under constant acceleration, the dependent variable y corresponds to velocity, m corresponds to acceleration, c corresponds to initial velocity and x, the independent variable, corresponds to time.

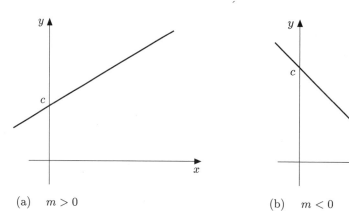

(a) $m > 0$ (b) $m < 0$

Figure 1.3

A linear model for a falling rock

The fact that linear functions arise in modelling the motion resulting from constant acceleration has been noted already. In Chapter C1, Section 4 you met several examples of mathematical models for the motion of falling objects. One example was concerned with the motion of a rock dislodged from the top of a cliff by a villain during the filming of a thriller. The film producer was interested in how long the rock would take to fall to the ground and how fast it would be travelling at ground impact. The velocity

($v\,\mathrm{m\,s^{-1}}$) of a rock, falling from the top of a cliff 35 m high, was modelled by the equation

$$v = 9.8t \qquad (0 \leq t \leq 2.7)$$

where t represented time in seconds after the rock starts to fall. The upper limit for t is the time at which the rock hits the ground. This linear function, describing the variation of velocity with time, results from integrating the constant function describing the rate of change of velocity with time starting from rest.

$$\frac{dv}{dt} = 9.8, \qquad (1.1)$$

$$\int \frac{dv}{dt}\,dt = v,$$

so, using the table of standard integrals in Chapter C2,

$$v = \int 9.8dt = 9.8t + c. \qquad (1.2)$$

In Chapter C1, the time at which the rock hits the ground (2.672 712 4 s) was stated more accurately, since its calculation was part of the stated purpose and it was to be used also to calculate velocity at ground impact.

In the chosen modelling context, $v = 0$ when $t = 0$, so $c = 0$ and this results in the required equation, $v = 9.8t$.

Remember that various assumptions are needed to obtain the quoted result of a linear variation in speed with time. It is assumed that there is no air resistance, no spinning and no wind.

Figure 1.4 shows v as a function of t. Velocity is a linearly increasing function of time and its graph is a straight line passing through $t = 0$, $v = 0$.

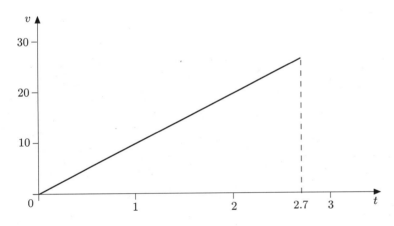

Figure 1.4

In which way should the equation for v be altered if the villain were to be a particularly strong example of the genre and able to *throw* the rock downwards at $5\,\mathrm{m\,s^{-1}}$? Remember from Chapter C1, Subsection 4.3, that, as long as we are measuring position or displacement downwards, a downward velocity is positive. Now we have $v = 5$ when $t = 0$. After substituting these values in $v = 9.8t + c$, we find that $c = 5$ or

$$v = 9.8t + 5 \qquad (0 \leq t \leq T_1),$$

where T_1 is the time at which the rock hits the ground when thrown downwards like this.

Since they are both downwards, the initial velocity simply adds to the velocity at any time resulting from falling under gravity.

Note that T_1 (instead of 2.7) is being used for the upper limit on t because we do not yet know what numerical value to assign to this quantity.

Activity 1.5   Expected values

(a) Will T_1 be more or less than 2.7?

(b) Sketch a graph of v for $(0 \leq t \leq T_1)$.

Comment

Solutions are given on page 65.

Consider now how the function for v will change if the villain is even mightier than we had previously thought and throws the rock *upwards* with an initial speed of $5\,\mathrm{m\,s^{-1}}$, instead of simply dislodging it or throwing it downwards. In this circumstance, the initial velocity is directed upwards, and position is being measured downwards, so the initial velocity is negative. We can use the equation $v = 9.8t + c$ again. This time $v = -5$ when $t = 0$, leading to $c = -5$ and

$$v = 9.8t - 5 \qquad (0 \leq t \leq T_2),$$

where the new time at which the rock hits the ground is denoted by T_2. The rock will rise before falling to the ground this time, so T_2 will be larger than T_1.

From the modelling point of view, there is one other significant time before the rock hits the ground. Figure 1.5 shows the new graph of v against t. Notice that there is a time at which v (which starts at -5) is zero. What does this mean?

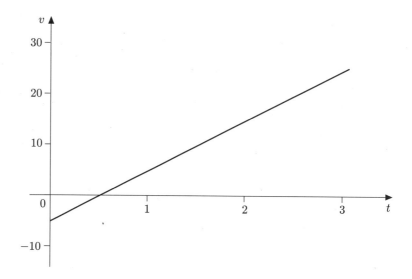

Figure 1.5

As time goes by, the fact that gravity is causing the rock to accelerate downwards means that the rock's upward motion will slow. Its velocity will decrease in magnitude until it reaches zero. At this particular instant the rock will be at its highest point and its velocity will change from upwards to downwards, passing instantaneously through zero in the process.

We can work out this time. We substitute zero for v and work out the corresponding t.

$$0 = 9.8t - 5,$$

so $t = \dfrac{5}{9.8} = 0.510\,204.$

This means that the rock is stationary about half a second after being thrown upwards.

Subsequently, the rock will fall until it hits the ground. But there is one more time that may be significant in the modelling context chosen here. During its journey to the ground 35 m beneath the cliff-top, the rock will pass the top of the cliff again. Note that we are modelling the motion of a particular point, say the lowest point, on the rock. A real rock, with appreciable size, will pass the top of the cliff, without landing on it or hitting it, only if it is thrown a little outwards as well as up.

Anyway, in principle we could use the function that we started with, representing the velocity of an object falling from rest under gravity, to work out how long the rock will take to pass the top of the cliff, having reached the highest point in its path. A simpler method is to argue that, as long as the rock is thrown from the cliff-top level (this requires the villain to be lying down!), the rock should take exactly the same time (approximately 0.5 s) to return to the level of the cliff-top as it took to rise above the cliff-top to the highest point in its path. So we simply double 0.5 s to deduce that the rock passes the cliff-top again about 1 s after being thrown.

Activity 1.6   Exploring variations

(a) Make your own sketch of Figure 1.5 and add lines to it to represent velocity as a function of time if the rock is:

   (i) thrown (downwards) with velocity $3 \, \text{m s}^{-1}$;

   (ii) thrown (upwards) with velocity $-2 \, \text{m s}^{-1}$.

(b) What do you deduce about the effect of the initial velocity on the graph of velocity against time?

(c) Imagine that the filming was on the moon with roughly one-sixth the gravitational pull of earth. Find a linear function that would describe the velocity of a dislodged rock in this new context.

(d) What do you deduce about the effect of changing the acceleration due to gravity on the graph of velocity against time?

Comment

Solutions are given on page 65.

So in the context of modelling motion under gravity, the *initial velocity* determines the vertical displacement of the line, its *intercept* on the v-axis, and the *acceleration* determines the *slope*. Again, given the modelling context, both of these influence the range of validity of the model, since they alter the time taken for the rock to reach the ground and this fixes the upper limit on time.

Like velocity, acceleration has direction as well as magnitude. As long as position is being measured downwards, and only gravity is considered to act, falling objects do not provide any examples of negative acceleration, but rocket motion does. Where downward accelerations are represented as positive, an upward acceleration will be negative. So a model of the motion of a rocket accelerating away from the earth could include a constant negative acceleration. Horizontal acceleration, say of a road vehicle, in the same direction as position is being measured, is represented as positive. Horizontal deceleration, for example when this vehicle is braking (as in Chapter C2), implies that velocity is decreasing with time, and is represented as negative. In mathematical modelling, it is usual to refer to *acceleration*, whether it represents acceleration or deceleration.

A linear model for a rocket taking off

Suppose that we are describing the motion of a rocket taking off vertically during its initial booster stage of 10 s. (By analogy with the falling rock model, we *might* model the acceleration as a constant $-20 \, \mathrm{m \, s^{-2}}$. The negative sign *would* arise because, in this model, downwards is positive and the acceleration is upwards. Since the rocket is starting from rest, an appropriate function would then be

$$v = -20t \qquad (0 \le t \le 10). \,)$$

However, in the context of a rocket it seems more natural to measure position upwards rather than downwards, so that the rocket's acceleration during its booster stage is $+20 \, \mathrm{m \, s^{-2}}$, and the corresponding function for velocity is

$$v = 20t \qquad (0 \le t \le 10). \tag{1.3}$$

This should describe the variation of its velocity with time until the end of the initial booster stage of its flight. Figure 1.6 shows the corresponding graph of velocity against time. Note the way in which the graph slopes upwards to the right. This function describes an increasingly positive velocity as time passes.

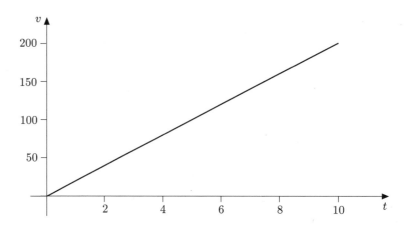

Figure 1.6

Suppose now that the booster stage finishes abruptly at ten seconds. The rocket will now be under the influence of the earth's gravity, so it will experience a downward acceleration of $9.8 \, \mathrm{m \, s^{-2}}$. What will be the function modelling the rocket's (upwardly measured) velocity during the *next* ten seconds?

Because position is measured upwards in this model, the acceleration is now negative, and equations (1.1) and (1.2) become

$$\frac{dv}{dt} = -9.8$$

$$v = \int -9.8 \, dt = -9.8t + c. \tag{1.4}$$

Activity 1.7 The rocket's motion after the booster stage

Use the information from the booster stage to find c, and thus write down the function for the velocity during the ten seconds after boost ceases.

Comment

The function we are looking for describes v during the time interval from $10\,\text{s}$ to $20\,\text{s}$, and so (by equation (1.4)) is of the form

$$v = -9.8t + c \qquad (10 \leq t \leq 20). \tag{1.5}$$

To find c, all we need to know is v at one point in this time interval. However, the beginning of the interval coincides with the end of the time interval for which we already know the function for v (see equation (1.3)). So, at time $t = 10$, the velocity is given using (1.3) by

$$v = 20 \times 10 = 200.$$

So, putting this value for v, and 10 for t, in equation (1.5), we have

$$200 = -9.8 \times 10 + c,$$
$$c = 298.$$

Finally, then, the velocity function in the ten seconds after boost ceases is

$$v = -9.8t + 298 \qquad (10 \leq t \leq 20).$$

Thus, the velocity function for the whole time interval from 0 to 20 seconds is

$$v = \begin{cases} 20t & (0 \leq t \leq 10) \\ -9.8t + 298 & (10 \leq t \leq 20). \end{cases}$$

The graph of this function is shown in Figure 1.7. Note the way in which the part which corresponds to the motion *after* the booster stage slopes downwards to the right, corresponding to negative acceleration.

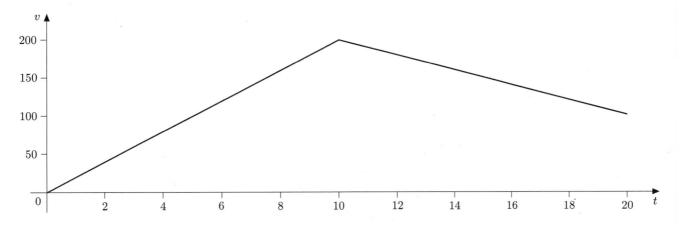

Figure 1.7

Activity 1.8   Motion of a satellite

(a) Imagine that a satellite is falling towards the earth at $5\,\mathrm{m\,s^{-1}}$ when a booster rocket is fired for $5\,\mathrm{s}$, accelerating it away from the earth at $10\,\mathrm{m\,s^{-2}}$. Write down a corresponding linear function that would describe its upward velocity during the booster stage.

(b) Sketch the corresponding graph of upward velocity against time.

(c) At what time would the upward velocity of the satellite be zero?

Comment

The solutions are given on page 66.

Other contexts for linear models

Linear functions may arise in contexts other than when modelling motion under constant acceleration, some of which you have met already. Calculating the amount of tape left on a cassette, garden border areas or populations are examples of such contexts. In each of these situations, the slope and intercept values will have some modelling significance. Indeed the behaviour and hence the suitability of a linear function of the form $y = mx + c$, when modelling any given situation, will be determined by the values of m and c.

Activity 1.9   Filling a rain-water barrel

During 20 minutes of rain, a cylindrical rain-water barrel that is initially empty is filled to a depth of $1.5\,\mathrm{cm}$.

(a) Choose variables to represent the level of water in the barrel and time.

Sketch a graph representing the level of water in the barrel if the intensity of rainfall remains constant over the 20-minute period.

(b) Write down a linear function that represents the level of water in the vessel together with its range of validity.

(c) State any assumptions that you have made.

(d) Write down the amended form of your answer to (b), if the vessel contains $2\,\mathrm{cm}$ of water initially and the depth *increases* by $1.5\,\mathrm{cm}$ during the 20 minutes.

Comment

The solutions are given on page 66.

Methods for calculating gradient

In Activity 1.9, it was fairly straightforward to work out the function since the intercept (0 or 2) was known already and the information for calculating the gradient ($1.5\,\mathrm{cm}$ in 20 minutes) was plain.

In another situation, you might be faced with two different pairs of values or *coordinates* with which to determine the parameters. From Chapter A3, Section 3, you may recall that two such points, or coordinate pairs, determine the line. Put another way, two pairs of values are needed to determine the two (unknown) parameters. Perhaps you have used this result already when carrying out Activity 1.9. The gradient, written as $\dfrac{1.5}{20}$ in the solution, may also be expressed as $\dfrac{1.5 - 0}{20 - 0}$ since the line connects the (time, level of water) coordinates $(20, 1.5)$ with $(0, 0)$.

In general the gradient is given by

$$\dfrac{\text{the change in the dependent variable}}{\text{the corresponding change in the independent variable}}$$

Once the gradient of the line has been calculated, it can be used with one of the known points to determine the intercept. If one of the points is $(0, 0)$, the intercept is zero.

Suppose that a new type of automatic car is being road tested. The test team want to know the maximum acceleration between 0 and $30\,\mathrm{m\,s^{-1}}$. They plan to calculate this by assuming that the acceleration is constant and measuring the time taken from rest to achieve a speed of $30\,\mathrm{m\,s^{-1}}$ at maximum acceleration. In their first test the speedometer reading is $30\,\mathrm{m\,s^{-1}}$ after $12\,\mathrm{s}$ from the start of timing and motion. We can think of these values in terms of (time, velocity) coordinates. At the start of timing the coordinates are $(0, 0)$. When the speedometer reads $30\,\mathrm{m\,s^{-1}}$ the coordinates are $(12, 30)$. If the acceleration is constant, then its magnitude will be given by the gradient of the line joining these two points. Using the 'change in variable' idea, the gradient is $\dfrac{30 - 0}{12 - 0} = 2.5$, and so the magnitude of the acceleration is $2.5\,\mathrm{m\,s^{-2}}$.

The 'change in variable' route to calculating the gradient is an abridged version of a more general method. The two pairs of coordinates may be used with the general equation of a line to work out the parameters of the particular line that passes through these two points.

The assumption of constant acceleration leads to a linear relationship between the velocity ($v\,\mathrm{m\,s^{-1}}$) and time ($t\,\mathrm{s}$) of the form

$$v = mt + c$$

where m and c are the parameters corresponding to gradient and intercept respectively.

The road test gives $v = 0$ when $t = 0$ and $v = 30$ when $t = 12$. These may be substituted into the general form to give

$$0 = 0 + c \tag{1.6}$$
$$30 = 12m + c. \tag{1.7}$$

You may recognise that these are simultaneous equations. Equation (1.6) gives $c = 0$, which may be substituted into equation (1.7) to give $m = 2.5$, corresponding to an acceleration of $2.5\,\mathrm{m\,s^{-2}}$, as before.

Suppose that the test team carry out a second test. In this test they note when speeds of $15\,\mathrm{m\,s^{-1}}$ and $27\,\mathrm{m\,s^{-1}}$ are reached and assume constant acceleration between *these* times and speeds. The speedometer reads $15\,\mathrm{m\,s^{-1}}$ after 4 seconds from the start of motion, and $27\,\mathrm{m\,s^{-1}}$ after $9\,\mathrm{s}$ from the start of motion. Let us use the general method on the data from this test. The (time, velocity) coordinates corresponding to the readings are $(4, 15)$ and $(9, 27)$. The equations resulting from substitutions in the general form are

$$15 = 4m + c \tag{1.8}$$
$$27 = 9m + c. \tag{1.9}$$

Here and throughout this chapter, 'intercept' will mean the intercept on the vertical axis, i.e. corresponding to the dependent variable.

$4m = 15 - c$

$m = \dfrac{15 - c}{4}$

$27 = 9\left(\dfrac{15 - c}{4}\right) + c$

$= \left(\dfrac{9 \times 15}{4}\right) - \dfrac{9}{4}c + c$

$\Rightarrow \dfrac{9}{4}c - c = \left(\dfrac{9 \times 15}{4}\right) - 27$

$\Rightarrow \dfrac{5}{4}c = 6\tfrac{3}{4} \quad \Rightarrow c = 6\tfrac{3}{4} \times \tfrac{4}{5} = 5.4$

$15 = 4m + c$

$27 = 9m + c$

$\Rightarrow \; 27 - 15 = (9m + c) - (4m + c)$

$\Rightarrow \; 12 = 9m - 4m$

$\Rightarrow \; 12 = 5m$

$m = \dfrac{12}{5} = 2.4$

We may subtract (1.8) from (1.9) to get rid of c:

$$27 - 15 = (9 - 4)m$$

or $\; m = 2.4$.

The resulting value of m may be substituted into either of the equations expressing the data to calculate c. Substituting into equation (1.8) gives $15 = 4 \times 2.4 + c$, or $c = 5.4$.

The resulting model is

$$v = 2.4t + 5.4 \qquad (4 \leq t \leq 9).$$

This model predicts an acceleration of $2.4\,\mathrm{m\,s^{-2}}$, which is fairly close to the previous result of $2.5\,\mathrm{m\,s^{-2}}$, but if we try to use this model at $t = 0$, what do we predict? The model predicts that $v = 5.4$ when $t = 0$. This is not consistent with $t = 0$ being the time at which the vehicle starts to move! So, even if the acceleration is constant between $15\,\mathrm{m\,s^{-1}}$ and $27\,\mathrm{m\,s^{-1}}$, it does not have the same values between $0\,\mathrm{m\,s^{-1}}$ and $15\,\mathrm{m\,s^{-1}}$ as between $15\,\mathrm{m\,s^{-1}}$ and $27\,\mathrm{m\,s^{-1}}$ or between $27\,\mathrm{m\,s^{-1}}$ and $30\,\mathrm{m\,s^{-1}}$, see Figure 1.8 which was drawn on the assumption that there was constant acceleration between $t = 0$ and $t = 4$ seconds and between $t = 9$ and $t = 12$ seconds.

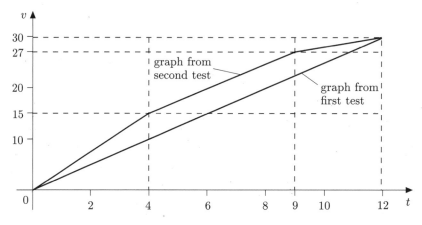

Figure 1.8:

A more general principle is illustrated by this example. It may be dangerous to use a model based on certain data at points other than those given by these data!

Data are plural.

The business of using a model outside the range of data for which it is known to be valid is called **extrapolation**. Use of the model between the data points on which it is based is called **interpolation** and it is used when we represent data by a continuous curve. In general, it may be said that it is risky to interpolate – and even riskier to extrapolate. Nevertheless, extrapolation or interpolation may be part of the purpose for a mathematical model in the first place.

The method just exemplified of finding gradient and intercept may be generalised. Suppose that we are specifying a linear function $y = mx + c$, where the dependent variable is y and the independent variable is x. We shall represent two known points by (p, q) and (r, s). The gradient, m, for the straight line, may be calculated either from $m = \dfrac{s - q}{r - p}$ or by substituting $y = q$ when $x = p$ and $y = s$ when $x = r$ in $y = mx + c$ to obtain two simultaneous equations. Subtraction of these eliminates c and allows m to be calculated. Then c, the intercept of the line on the y-axis, may be found by substitution in $y = mx + c$, either putting $x = p$ and $y = q$ or putting $x = r$ and $y = s$.

Activity 1.10   Interpolating

Use the general method to deduce the different accelerations (assuming that they are constant) between the start of motion and a velocity of $15\,\mathrm{m\,s^{-1}}$, and between the velocities of $27\,\mathrm{m\,s^{-1}}$ and $30\,\mathrm{m\,s^{-1}}$.

Handwritten:
$(0,0)\quad (4,15)$
$y = mx + c \qquad 15 = m4$
$0 = m0 + c \Rightarrow m = \frac{15}{4}$
$\Rightarrow c = 0$

$(9, 27)\quad (12, 30)$
$27 = 9m + c$
$30 = 12m + c$
$\Rightarrow 30 - 27 = (12 - 9)\,m$
$\Rightarrow 3m = 3 \qquad m = 1$

Comment

The solution is given on page 66.

Linear functions may be useful in economics. A lot of attention is paid to the way in which *demand* for a product varies with its price. A measure of demand is the number of items sold, if available, in a given period. You may remember the modelling context in Chapter C1, where the purpose was to determine the best price for the product of a cottage industry, given certain details about costs and with certain assumptions about the way the number of items sold per month varied with price. The price affects the profit and hence, in turn, the number manufactured in response to the demand. The number of items manufactured in a given period is known as the *supply*. Information about the variation of demand or supply with price may be obtained from market surveys. Constant functions are not appropriate in this context, since both demand and supply vary with price. In the absence of other information, the simplest way to model the variation of either demand or supply with price is to use a linear function.

Activity 1.11   Relating demand to price

When the price of a luxury consumer item is £1000, a market survey reveals that the demand is 100 000 items per year. Another survey has shown that at a price of £600, the demand for the item is 200 000 items per year. Assuming that both surveys are valid, find a linear function that relates demand Q to price P. What demand would be predicted by the linear function at a price of £750? What demand would be predicted at a price of £500? Comment on the validity of both predictions.

Handwritten:
Range!
$600 \le P \le 1000$
$(1000, 100\,000)$
$(600, 200\,000)$
$Q = mP + c$
$100\,000 = 1000\,m + c \qquad 200\,000 = 600\,m + c$
$200\,000 - 100\,000 = (600 - 1000)\,m$
$\Rightarrow -400\,m = 100\,000$
$\Rightarrow m = -250$
$200\,000 = 600 \times -250 + c$
$\Rightarrow c = 200\,000 + 150\,000$
$= 350\,000$
Particular solution
$Q = -250P + 350\,000$
£750
$Q = (-250 \times 750) + 350\,000$
$= 162\,500$

Comment

The solution is given on page 66.

Activity 1.12   Checking terms

Before leaving this section, you may find it useful to check your understanding of the terms used. Do you know what they mean and are you confident that you can use them appropriately? Check where they are to be found in the course Handbook and whether you need to add any annotations.

Comment

It may be useful to continue this checking as you work through the rest of the chapter.

Activity 1.13   Tabulated summaries

As part of summarising this unit in a form that may be useful to you subsequently, we want you to start a table or series of tables about the properties of functions and their applications. A suggested form for the first few entries in this table is shown below. You will be asked to complete later entries as part of a continuation of this activity. The final complete version of the table will be part of your own summary of the chapter. When copying the entries given below and at the end of Sections 2, 3 and 4 into your own version of the table, feel free to alter the contents to suit what is most helpful for you. You may prefer to use different symbols from those given, or you may prefer different sketches from those given. You may wish to add examples of other modelling contexts or, indeed, to cite ones different from those listed.

Table 1.1

Behaviour	Formula for function	Attributes	Sketch of function	Some modelling contexts
Constant over some range of the independent variable	$y = c$ $(A \leq x \leq B)$	Gradient $\left(\dfrac{dy}{dx}\right)$ is zero	$c > 0$	Motion under constant acceleration for a certain period. Fixed rate mortgages. Road widths.
Linear increase	$y = mx + c$ $(A \leq x \leq B)$ $m > 0$	At $x = 0$, $y = c$ constant gradient $\dfrac{dy}{dx} = m$ for $(A \leq x \leq B)$	$m > 0$	Velocity during motion under constant acceleration. Depth of water in a container during constant intensity rainfall.
Linear decrease	$y = mx + c$ $(A \leq x \leq B)$ $m < 0$	At $x = 0$, $y = c$ constant gradient $\dfrac{dy}{dx} = m$ for $(A \leq x \leq B)$	$m < 0$	Variation of demand for an item with price.

Summary of Section 1

◇   In this section, it has been pointed out that Step 2 of the mathematical modelling cycle may involve choosing an appropriate function that behaves in the relevant manner and which is as simple as possible. Constant functions or linear functions may be appropriate in some contexts. It is important to express the range of validity by specifying the domain of the function. Step 3 may involve finding the parameter values that specify the function.

◇   The assumption that a quantity is constant leads to horizontal straight-line graphs for the quantity and zero derivatives. The assumption that the rate of change of a quantity is constant leads to a linear function for the quantity and a zero second derivative of the quantity. For example, the assumption of constant acceleration leads to a linear function for velocity.

◇   Both acceleration and velocity are vectors. They have direction as well as magnitude. When considering the motion of falling objects with position measured downwards, downward acceleration is positive while upward velocities and accelerations are negative. The opposite is true when position is measured upwards. Horizontal acceleration in direction of increasing position is positive, while deceleration is negative.

◇   A modelling context in which linear functions may be appropriate is the variation of supply or demand with price.

◇   The gradient of a linear function may be deduced from two points either by using

$$\frac{\text{the change in the dependent variable}}{\text{the corresponding change in the independent variable}}$$

or by setting up two simultaneous equations. The gradient may be used with one of the points or one of the equations to determine the intercept.

◇   It may be risky to extrapolate a model based on data outside the range of these data or to interpolate between data points. (Extrapolation is generally riskier than interpolation.) However, either extrapolation or interpolation may be part of the original purpose of a model.

Exercises for Section 1

Exercise 1.1

The gradient of a hill is described as 1 in 4.

(a) What kind of model for the relationship between distance and height is implied here?

(b) What would be the range of validity of the model?

Exercise 1.2

Rain is falling steadily on a roof at a rate of $0.001 \, \text{m}^3$ per minute, over a period of two hours, and the run-off is collected in a gutter which runs into a rain-water barrel.

(a) Write down a model for the relationship between the height of rain-water (h m) collected in the barrel and time (t minutes), assuming that the base of the barrel has an area of $0.2 \, \text{m}^2$.

(b) What assumption(s) have you made?

Exercise 1.3

Your oil tank holds 1000 litres of oil. Your average oil consumption is 120 litres per week. Write down a model for the relationship between the volume of oil in the tank and time. What would be the range of validity of the model?

2 Quadratic functions

2.1 Quadratic functions and parabolas

Activity 2.1 Recalling quadratics

Look back at Chapter A4 and the associated sections of Computer Book A.

(a) How were quadratic functions introduced in a modelling context?

(b) Write down three general forms for quadratic functions.

Comment

(a) Chapter A4 introduced quadratic functions when modelling the area of a square and the width of exhibits in an exhibition hall consistent with fire regulations.

(b) The computer work for Chapter A4 emphasised that any quadratic function can be written in either of the forms

$$f(x) = ax^2 + bx + c,$$
$$f(x) = a(x - b)^2 + c.$$

In addition, if a quadratic function has one or more zeros, it may be written in the form

$$f(x) = a(x - b)(x - c).$$

In this chapter we shall use the first two of these three forms. To help to distinguish between them, we shall use capital letters for the parameters of the second form. Thus, we shall consider quadratic functions of the forms

We use y rather than $f(x)$ for ease of manipulation.

$$y = ax^2 + bx + c,$$
$$y = A(x - B)^2 + C.$$

The latter is often expressed more conveniently as

$$y - C = A(x - B)^2.$$

Graphs of y against x resulting from these general forms of quadratic functions are called **parabolas**. The coefficients a, b and c or A, B and C influence the shape, form and position of the graph of the associated parabola. They are the **parameters** of the parabola. In particular, a or A determines how wide the parabola opens (large a or A implies a narrow parabola, small a or A implies a wide parabola) and whether it has a lowest or highest point (negative a or A implies a parabola with a highest point). The form $y - C = A(x - B)^2$ is the most useful form for determining the graphical appearance of a parabola (see Figure 2.1). It enables the coordinates of the highest or lowest point, known as the **vertex**, to be written down immediately. The coordinates of the vertex are given by (B, C). Changing the value of B shifts the vertex, and hence the whole parabola, to the left or right. Changing the value of C shifts the vertex, and hence the whole parabola, up or down.

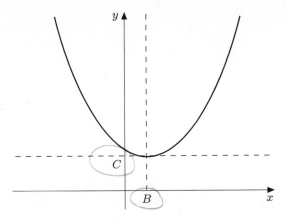

Figure 2.1

Activity 2.2   Recognising quadratics

One of the functions chosen in Chapter C1, Section 1 to describe the variation of jogger Mary's location with time was a quadratic function:

$$s = \frac{t^2}{9} \quad (0 \le t \le 30). \tag{2.1}$$

Compare function (2.1) with the general form $y - C = A(x - B)^2$.

(a) Which variables correspond to y and x in this case? $y = s \quad t = x$.

(b) What are the values of C, A and B? $s - O = \frac{1}{9}(t^2 - o)^2$

Comment

The solutions are given on page 67.

$C = 0$
$A = 1/9$
$B = 0$

2.2 Modelling with parabolas

The function

$$s = \frac{t^2}{9} \quad (0 \le t \le 30),$$

used in Chapter C1 to describe the variation of jogger Mary's location with time, represents part of a parabola starting at the *origin* ($s = 0$ and $t = 0$) and rising to $s = 100$ at the end of its range of validity ($t = 30$). In the context described in Chapter C1, 'negative' times correspond to times before the jogging friends (Mary, Jenny and Tom) meet at one end of the street, and were not considered. What would this parabolic function have predicted if it were valid for Mary's location up to 30 s *before* the meeting of joggers? The answer to this can be deduced from the graph of the function for $(-30 \le t \le 30)$ shown in Figure 2.2.

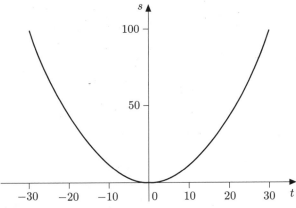

Figure 2.2

23

The parabolic form predicts that at $t = -30$, Mary was 100 m away at the other end of the street and for $(-30 \leq t \leq 0)$ she was moving towards the end at which the joggers met. Chapter C1 explained that velocity is given by the rate of change of position. The rate of change of position, or instantaneous velocity, is given by the gradient of the position–time graph. Since the gradient of the parabola for s is steeper near $t = -30$ than near $t = 0$, the chosen function for s and new range of validity suggest that Mary was running fast at one end of the street, where we started timing at $t = -30$, slowed down on approaching the end, where she met the other joggers, and then ran back up the street accelerating as she did so. Note that the velocity (gradient) for $(-30 \leq t \leq 0)$ is negative while for $(0 \leq t \leq 30)$ it is positive. This is consistent with the change in direction at $t = 0$.

You met this context in Subsection 1.2 of this chapter and in Chapter C1, Subsection 4.3.

Let us consider falling objects again and return to the context of the thriller film and the villain on the cliff-top dislodging a rock. Suppose that, as film director, you are considering a variation of the plot whereby the rock hits the roof of a vehicle carrying the hero and heroine, instead of the ground. This means that you may be interested in the position as well as the velocity of the rock at any time. We can start from the linear function relating velocity and time for the dislodged rock,

$$v = 9.8t \qquad (0 \leq t \leq T)$$

where T represents the time at which the rock hits the roof of the vehicle. The precise value of T will depend upon the height of the vehicle.

We know from Chapter C1 that velocity is the derivative of position with respect to time, i.e. $v = \dfrac{ds}{dt}$, where s is the position of the rock measured from the cliff-top. So $\dfrac{ds}{dt} = 9.8t$, which is a first order differential equation, and we can obtain an expression for s by use of the table of standard integrals in Chapter C2. This gives

$$s = \frac{9.8}{2}t^2 + c = 4.9t^2 + c.$$

$s = 4.9t^2$ is quoted in Chapter C1, Subsection 4.3 as the result of a standard model, $s = \frac{1}{2}gt^2$, for falling objects.

If s is measured *from* the cliff-top and timing starts with release of the rock, then $s = 0$ when $t = 0$, so $c = 0$. The resulting function is

$$s = 4.9t^2 \qquad (0 \leq t \leq T). \tag{2.2}$$

Activity 2.3   Sketching a function

(a) What kind of function is function (2.2)?

(b) If the vehicle roof is 2 m above the ground and the cliff-top is 35 m above the ground, calculate a value for T.

(c) Given this value for T, sketch the function.

Comment

The solutions are on page 67.

In this modelling context, negative time would correspond to time before the villain dislodges the rock. It seems likely that the rock would be stationary before this instant. The parabolic function would not be appropriate for $t < 0$, since it would predict that s was positive and the rock had been rising from the ground towards the cliff-top just before $t = 0$. An appropriate function would have two parts to its domain.

For $t \leq 0$, s would be constant at zero, and for $(0 < t \leq T)$, $s = 4.9t^2$. The corresponding graph would also have two parts: a flat line along the t-axis for $t \leq 0$ and part of a parabola for $0 < t \leq T$.

You may recall that in Section 4 of Chapter C1, a different form of quadratic function for position was appropriate if position was measured *upwards* as height (h) above the ground. This was given as

$$h = 35 - 4.9t^2 \qquad (0 \leq t \leq 2.7). \qquad (2.3)$$

When position is measured upwards, velocities and accelerations which are downwards, which would be the case for falling objects, will be negative.

Note that it is possible to find an appropriate function that has more than one part. You have already seen an example of such a function in Section 1; namely the function describing the velocity of a rocket during and after its booster stage.

Activity 2.4   Which way up?

(a) By comparing function (2.3) with $y = ax^2 + bx + c$, deduce values for a, b and c and determine whether the parabola corresponding to function (2.3) has a highest or lowest point.

(b) Write down an appropriate function for the variation of h with t if height is measured upwards from the top of a 2 m-high vehicle.

(c) Sketch the function in (b).

$h = 35 - 4.9t^2$
$\Rightarrow h = -4.9t^2 + 35.$
$\Rightarrow a$ is negative
and parabola has a highest point

Comment

The solutions are given on page 67.

Consider again the situation in which position is measured downwards from the cliff-top, but the villain is lying down on the cliff-top and throws the rock *upwards* with velocity $5\,\mathrm{m\,s^{-1}}$. In Subsection 1.2 an appropriate linear function for velocity was given as

$$v = 9.8t - 5 \qquad (0 \leq t \leq T).$$

Using $v = \dfrac{ds}{dt}$ again,

$$\frac{ds}{dt} = 9.8t - 5 \qquad (0 \leq t \leq T),$$

and integrating this first order differential equation directly by means of the table of standard integrals gives

$$s = 4.9t^2 - 5t + c$$

where c is an arbitrary constant.

If s is measured downwards from the top of the cliff, then when $t = 0$, $s = 0$. Substituting these values in the quadratic equation gives $c = 0$.

The appropriate quadratic function for s is therefore

$$s = 4.9t^2 - 5t \qquad (0 \leq t \leq T).$$

The nature of this quadratic function is such that for a given value of s there are two possible values of t.

25

If we write the function in a slightly different way, taking out a common factor of t on the right-hand side of the equation,

$$s = t(4.9t - 5) \qquad (0 \le t \le T),$$

then it is possible to see, for example, that $s = 0$ at two different times. These are when $t = 0$ *and* when the expression in the bracket is zero. The first possibility is consistent with the initial position of the rock. The second possibility gives $t = \dfrac{5}{4.9}$, which is a little more than 1 and is the same as the value we deduced, in Subsection 1.2, by doubling the time we had calculated for the rock to reach the zero velocity position. This confirms the earlier reasoning.

The rock will be at the cliff-top level at two different times. It is there at the instant when it is thrown. It rises until its velocity is zero and then descends, passing cliff-top level again on its way to impact with the ground or with the vehicle roof. Since the initial motion of the rock is upwards and position is defined as positive downwards, the initial part of the rock's path corresponds to negative s. The parabola associated with the appropriate function crosses the $s = 0$ axis twice and has a vertex at which s is negative. A sketch of s against t for this case is shown in Figure 2.3.

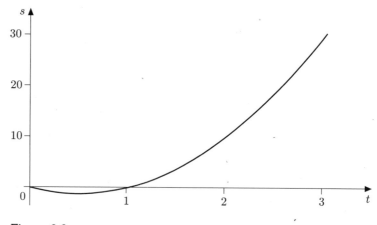

Figure 2.3

Activity 2.5   How high does it go?

(a) How high does the rock rise after being thrown upwards at $5\,\mathrm{m\,s}^{-1}$? (*Hint*: use the previously determined value of the time when the rock reaches its highest point.)

(b) Find a quadratic function that would be appropriate for the position of the rock if it were measured in terms of height above ground level.

Comment

Solutions are given on page 67.

Activity 2.6   Making choices

(a) Note that the form of the parabola makes it inevitable that, as long as it is plotted over a sufficiently wide range, and apart from its vertex, there will always be two values on the curve for each value of one of the variables. Which of these values make sense in a mathematical model will depend on the modelling context. In each of the contexts mentioned so far in this section, describe how each context has determined the part of the parabola that is of interest and hence the range being considered.

(b) Note also that there is a connection between the vertex on a parabola and the point where the gradient of that parabola is zero. In fact these points are the same! Write down your thoughts on the modelling significance of such points on the parabolas resulting from the 'falling rock' contexts.

(c) Can you say how your comments could affect the choices you make in other modelling situations?

You may find it useful to record your ideas in your Learning File. A sheet is provided for this purpose.

If you are interleaving your computing work with your study of the main text, this would be a convenient point at which to start work on Chapter C3, Section 5 of Computer Book C and work through Subsection 5.1.

2.3   Parabolas and optimisation

Because the vertex may represent a highest or lowest point, a quadratic function may be the appropriate type of function to choose in a modelling problem where a maximum or a minimum is involved (optimisation problems, for example). Chapter C1, Section 5 explored the problem of working out the selling price for the product of a cottage industry that would maximise the profit, given certain details of, or assumptions about, costs and market behaviour. One of the functions, derived in that chapter and relating profit ($£M$) to price ($£P$), was

$$M = -10P^2 + 320P - 2420 \qquad (12 \le P \le 20). \qquad (2.4)$$

This resulted from an assumed linear variation with number of items sold per month (demand) with price.

You will notice that this is a quadratic function. By comparing this function with the form $y = ax^2 + bx + c$ it is possible to decide whether the corresponding parabola, which would result from graphing M against P, would open upwards or downwards. Here M corresponds to y and P to x. The coefficient corresponding to a in the general form is -10. This is negative, so the resulting parabola will open downwards. In other words it will have a *highest point* or *maximum* for some value of P. This is comforting in the context of a *maximisation* or optimisation problem!

We can go further in specifying the resulting parabola by reference to the other general form: $y - C = A(x - B)^2$. If we multiply out the bracket on the right-hand side we get

Recall *completing the square* in Chapter A3.

$$y - C = Ax^2 - 2ABx + AB^2$$

or

$$y = Ax^2 - 2ABx + AB^2 + C.$$

Compare this general form with the function (2.4) relating profit and price for the cottage industry:

$$\begin{array}{ccccc} y & = & Ax^2 & -2ABx & +AB^2 + C \\ & & \downarrow & \downarrow & \downarrow \\ M & = & -10P^2 & +320P & -2420 \end{array}$$

Using the equivalences suggested by the arrows, we are able to write down that

$$A = -10 \tag{2.5}$$
$$2AB = -320 \tag{2.6}$$
$$AB^2 + C = -2420. \tag{2.7}$$

These are three equations for three unknowns.

Putting $A = -10$ in equation (2.6) gives $B = 16$. Putting $A = -10$ and $B = 16$ in equation (2.7) gives

$$-2560 + C = -2420,$$

and so

$$C = 140.$$

This means that the equation for M may also be written in the form

$$M - 140 = -10(P - 16)^2, \tag{2.8}$$

corresponding to the general form $y - C = A(x - B)^2$.

In the general form, C corresponds to the value of y at the vertex of the parabola. Since y in the general form corresponds to M in the current modelling context, we deduce that $M = 140$ at the highest point on the parabola. B represents the value of x at the lowest or highest point of the general parabola. Here x corresponds to P, so we deduce that $P = 16$ at the vertex of the parabola corresponding to the function relating profit and price. These deductions mean that a maximum profit of £140 is obtained when the price is £16. In Chapter C1, this result was obtained by finding where the derivative or derived function of the function is zero. We can call this the *differentiation* method. Our work at this point shows that there is another way based on examination of the properties of the quadratic. The alternative to the differentiation method requires finding the location of the vertex of the relevant parabola. When you come to do the computer activity associated with this chapter, you will realise that you could do this fairly painlessly (without any calculus *or* algebra) by means of Mathcad and the zoom facility.

Activity 2.7   Ways of maximising

Reflect on the connection between what was pointed out in Activity 2.6(b) and the previous paragraph above.

Comment

The method used in Chapter C1 to find the maximum profit was to look for the price that made the derivative of profit with respect to price equal to zero. This is equivalent to finding the highest point on the corresponding curve of profit against price. So the differentiation method and the method introduced here find the same thing.

2.4 Finding the equation of a parabola

Let us think back to the joggers' example first introduced in Chapter C1 and pursued at the start of this section. Suppose that there is another jogger, Dick, who starts at the same time from his house halfway along the street, in other words 50 m from the end of the street at which the others start. Like Mary, Dick accelerates at a constant rate as he jogs, but his acceleration is less than Mary's so that he is caught up by Mary at the other end of the street. What would be an appropriate parabolic function that could be used to model the variation of Dick's position with time?

Figure 2.2 shows the parabola appropriate to Mary's motion. To represent Dick's motion, we need part of another parabola that has its vertex at $s = 50$ when $t = 0$ and rises to $s = 100$ when $t = 30$. The vertex will correspond to Dick's starting point, since the gradient of the parabola is zero at the vertex, and it will be consistent with zero velocity at the ← *assuming Dick has zero velocity at start of run.* vertex. In coordinate terms, we need the equation of a parabola that has its lowest point or vertex at $(0, 50)$ and passes through $(30, 100)$.

The general form

$$y - C = A(x - B)^2$$

is useful here.

In this case y corresponds to s and x to t. So the equation relating s and t is

$$s - C = A(t - B)^2.$$

According to the general form the coordinates of the vertex are (B, C). We know that the coordinates of the vertex are $(0, 50)$. So we can deduce that $B = 0$ and $C = 50$. It remains only to find A. The fact that the parabola must pass through $(30, 100)$ may be used for this purpose. These values together with those for B and C may be substituted in the general equation.

$$100 - 50 = A(30 - 0)^2$$

so $50 = 900A$ or $A = \frac{1}{18}$,

and the function we want is

$$s = 50 + \frac{1}{18}t^2 \qquad (0 \le t \le 30).$$

Note that the coefficient of t^2, corresponding to A in the second general form for the parabola, is less in this case than in the equation for the parabola representing Mary's jogging where it was $1/9$. This means that the parabola is wider or flatter. These two parabolas are shown together in Figure 2.4.

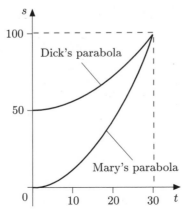

Figure 2.4

Coordinates of vertex
$(0,2) = (B, C)$
So $B = 0$, $C = 2$
Substituting in general
form $y - C = A(x - B)^2$
gives $y - 2 = A(x - 0)^2$
$\Rightarrow y = Ax^2 + 2$
using values $(4, 4)$
$4 = 4^2 A + 2$
$\Rightarrow 16A = 2$
$A = \frac{1}{8}$
So equation is
$y = \frac{1}{8}x^2 + 2$

Activity 2.8   Finding the equation

Find the equation of a parabola with vertex at $(0, 2)$ and passing through the point $(4, 4)$.

Comment

The solution is given on page 68.

Activity 2.9   Summarising Section 2

A suggested form for the next few rows of the summary table is shown below. These rows are not complete. You should try to complete these rows as part of this activity. The final complete version of the table will be part of your own summary of the chapter. Feel free to alter the contents to suit what is most helpful for you. You might prefer to use different symbols from the ones given or you may wish to add examples of other modelling contexts or, indeed, to cite different ones from those listed.

You may wish to add to your comments for Activity 1.13.

Table 2.1

Behaviour	Formula for function	Attributes	Sketch of function	Some modelling contexts
Quadratic increase	$y - C = A(x - B)^2$ for $x \geq B$	For $A > 0$ upward opening, vertex at (B, C)		Position of object moving with constant acceleration
Quadratic decrease	$y - C = A(x - B)^2$ for $x \geq B$	for $A < 0$ downward opening, vertex at (B, C)		

Summary of Section 2

◇   The functions that arise in modelling the position of an object moving under constant acceleration are quadratic. The function that arises in relating profit to price after assuming linear relationships between demand and supply and demand and price, is quadratic. Quadratic functions can be used to model non-linear increases or decreases, or situations involving a single maximum or minimum.

◇   The curve resulting from a quadratic function is called a parabola. Its lowest or highest point is called its vertex and corresponds to zero gradient. An alternative to the differentiation method of finding the maximum or minimum of a function is to locate its highest or lowest point, e.g. in the case of a quadratic function, the vertex of the corresponding parabola.

Exercises for Section 2

Exercise 2.1

Returning to the thriller context, suppose the heroine is driving a double-decker bus 4 metres high. Use equation (2.3) to estimate how long it would take for the rock to hit the roof of the bus after being dislodged.

Exercise 2.2

When a ball is thrown as a projectile, which of the following statements are true at the highest point of its path?

(a) The horizontal velocity component is zero.

(b) The horizontal acceleration component is zero.

(c) The vertical velocity component is zero.

(d) The vertical acceleration component is zero.   *see note p2 stop press 3.*

Exercise 2.3

Imagine that you are an ice-cream seller (of cones only) on a hot day and that from experience you expect to sell 1000 cones during your working day between 10 am and 6 pm.

(a) Set up a parabolic model for the *rate* at which customers buy cones by using the expected location of the vertex of the parabola.

(b) Use a known end-point of the parabola to find a relationship between the parameter that controls the rate of opening of the parabola and the maximum rate of selling.

(c) On the basis of the area enclosed between this parabola and the time axis on a graph, predict the maximum rate at which cones will be bought.

(d) State any assumptions that you have made.

quantity Q (vertical axis), *time t* (horizontal axis)

$$y - C = A(x - B)^2 \qquad y = Q, \; x = t$$
at the vertex B, C $\qquad C = Q_{max}$

3 Other non-linear functions

3.1 Exponential increase

Activity 3.1   Recalling exponentials

(a) Look back at Subsection 7.2 of Chapter A4 to ascertain the definition of an exponential function and the natural exponential function.

(b) List some examples from Chapters A4 and C1 of modelling contexts in which exponential functions are appropriate.

(c) What special property of the exponential function is introduced in Chapter C2?

Comment

(a) An exponential function has the form $y = a^x$ where $a > 0$. The natural exponential function has the form $y = e^x$ where $e = 2.718\,282\ldots$.

(b) In Chapter A4, exponential functions arose when modelling compound interest and mortgages. The natural exponential function was found to be appropriate when modelling language divergence. Chapter C1 used exponential functions when modelling cottage industry profits and used car finances.

(c) Chapter C2, Subsection 3.3 pointed out that a special property of exponential functions, for example $P = \exp(kt)$, is that the rate of change of the function P at any given value of P is directly proportional to that value. This can be expressed by the differential equation

$$\frac{dP}{dt} = kP. \tag{3.1}$$

You should be able to use the table of standard derivatives in Chapter C1 to check for yourself that $P = \exp(kt)$ is a solution to this differential equation.

Let us look at a specific example of the exponential function used for a model of population increase.

A large city (or a small country!) could have a population which has been estimated at 12 000 000 and is assumed to be growing at about 1% per year. The discussion in Subsection 7.5 of Chapter A4 suggests that, in that case, a suitable population model could be

The context in Chapter A4 was one of the rate of divergence of languages, but the principle of using exponential functions is the same.

$$P = 12\,000\,000\exp(0.01t) \qquad (0 \le t \le 10) \tag{3.2}$$

where P is the number in the population at time t in years.

Activity 3.2 A model for population growth

(a) What does function (3.2) imply about the population when $t = 0$?

(b) Which factor apart from the *initial population* determines how fast the population is growing?

(c) What is the range of validity?

(d) What does function (3.2) imply about values of P for $t > 0$?

Comment

The solutions are given on page 68.

A rearrangement of equation (3.1) is

$$\frac{1}{P}\frac{dP}{dt} = k \qquad (P \neq 0) \tag{3.3}$$

where P represents population and t represents time. This means that the rate of change of population at some instant divided by the population at that instant (or, in other words, the *fractional* or *proportional* rate of change of population) is constant and the constant value, k, is called the **instantaneous fractional** (or **proportional**) **growth rate**.

A general form of exponential function for use in modelling population is

$$P = P_0 \exp(kt) \qquad (P_0 > 0)$$

where P_0 is the initial population – that is, the value of P at $t = 0$. A diagram of the function is shown in Figure 3.1 for $k > 0$.

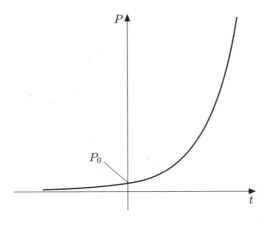

Figure 3.1

Note that as t becomes large and positive, P becomes very large. Normally such a population model would be used to predict values of P for $t > 0$, where $t = 0$ represents the present (or some time at which the population is known). In Figure 3.1, however, values of P are shown for $t < 0$. These correspond to extrapolation of the model into the past. Note that as t becomes increasingly negative, P becomes very small but is never zero or negative. Indeed, $\exp(x)$ is positive for any value of x.

Remember that $\exp(x)$ is another way of writing e^x.

Since $\dfrac{dP}{dt} = kP$, and $\dfrac{dP}{dt}$ is the rate at which P is increasing with time, an increase or decrease in the value of P will result in an increase or decrease in the rate at which the function increases. At a given value of P, say

33

$P = P_0$, $\dfrac{dP}{dt} = kP_0$ represents the rate at which the population is increasing, when $P = P_0$. This rate is increased if *either* k or P_0 is increased.

Let us consider again the specific example (3.2):

$$P = 12\,000\,000 \exp(0.01t) \qquad (0 \le t \le 10).$$

Here P_0 is $12\,000\,000$ and k is 0.01. The rate at which the population described by this model is growing at $t = 0$ is given by $12\,000\,000 \times 0.01 = 120\,000$ individuals per year. If the population at $t = 0$ is doubled so that the appropriate function is

$$P = 24\,000\,000 \exp(0.01t) \qquad (0 \le t \le 10), \tag{3.4}$$

then the rate of growth at $t = 0$ is $24\,000\,000 \times 0.01 = 240\,000$ individuals per year. Doubling P_0 results in doubling the rate of growth even though k (0.01 in this case) has been kept constant.

If, instead, the instantaneous fractional growth rate (k) is doubled from 0.01 to 0.02, while keeping the given initial population, then the appropriate function is

$$P = 12\,000\,000 \exp(0.02t), \tag{3.5}$$

and the rate of change of population at $t = 0$ becomes $12\,000\,000 \times 0.02 = 240\,000$ individuals per year. This is the same as for function (3.4). However, function (3.5), with $k = 0.02$, implies a faster growth for $t > 0$ than function (3.4). This is clear in Figure 3.2, which shows the three functions 3.2, 3.4 and 3.5 extrapolated as far as $t = 70$.

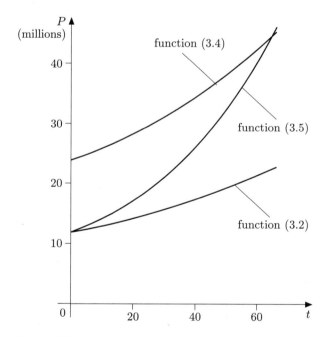

Figure 3.2

The exponential function may be used in models for other types of growth as well as population growth. A general form may be written

$$y = a \exp(bx) \qquad (c \le x \le d), \tag{3.6}$$

where a represents the value of y at $x = 0$. Here, a is the intercept on the y-axis of a graphical representation of the function, while b controls the rate of growth and c and d represent limits on x.

In this general form, a and b represent the **parameters** of the exponential function, which can be selected to fit any given modelling situation where an exponential function may be an appropriate choice.

3.2 Linearisation of exponential functions

The question arises as to how the parameters of an exponential function might be found from given data. A useful technique for doing this follows from the fact that it is possible to 'undo' an exponential function and convert it into a linear function by composing it with the logarithm function (which is the inverse of the function exp). Before going into the details of this process, it is worth recalling some useful rules for manipulating exponentials and logarithms, and making connections between them.

Table 3.1   Rules for manipulating exponentials

Rule 1	$\exp a \times \exp b = \exp(a + b)$	$(a, b \text{ in } \mathbb{R})$
Rule 2	$\dfrac{\exp a}{\exp b} = \exp(a - b)$	$(a, b \text{ in } \mathbb{R})$
Rule 3	$(\exp a)^b = \exp(ab)$	$(a, b \text{ in } \mathbb{R})$
Rule 4	$\exp 0 = 1$	
Rule 5	$(\exp a)^0 = 1$	$(a \text{ in } \mathbb{R})$
Rule 6	$\exp 1 = e$	

Table 3.2   Rules for manipulating logarithms

Rule 1	$\ln a + \ln b = \ln(ab)$	$(a, b > 0)$
Rule 2	$\ln a - \ln b = \ln\left(\dfrac{a}{b}\right)$	$(a, b > 0)$
Rule 3	$\ln(a^b) = b \ln a$	$(a > 0, \ b \text{ in } \mathbb{R})$
Rule 4	$\ln 1 = 0$	

these also apply to $\log_{10}$

Table 3.3   Connection and interpretation rules

Rule 1	$\log_{10} a = \dfrac{\ln a}{\ln 10}$	$(a > 0)$

[This rule can be generalised to $\log_c(a) = \dfrac{\ln(a)}{\ln(c)}$ for any $c > 1$.]

Rule 2a	$\ln(\exp a) = a$	$(a \text{ in } \mathbb{R})$
Rule 2b	$\exp(\ln a) = a$	$(a > 0)$
Rule 3a	$\log_{10}(10^a) = a$	$(a \text{ in } \mathbb{R})$
Rule 3b	$10^{\log_{10}(a)} = a$	$(a > 0)$

[This rule can be generalised like Rule 1, by replacing 10 by any $c > 1$.]

Rule 4	$p^a = e^{ka}$ where $k = \ln p$	$(a \text{ in } \mathbb{R}, p > 0)$

Notes

(a) Rule 1 of Table 3.3 shows that natural logarithms and logarithms to a different base are related by a multiplying factor that depends only on the base. This means that Rules 1 to 4 in Table 3.2 remain valid when the natural logarithm is replaced by the logarithm to some fixed base. For example,

$$\log_{10} a + \log_{10} b = \log_{10}(ab).$$

(b) Rule 2 of Table 3.3 is an expression of the fact that exp has domain $\mathbb{R}$ and codomain $(0, \infty)$ while ln has domain $(0, \infty)$ and codomain $\mathbb{R}$, and each is the other's inverse.

Let us try 'undoing' the exponential in the particular example (3.5):

$$P = 12\,000\,000 \exp(0.02t).$$

Since both sides of the equation are equal, the natural logarithms of both sides are also equal. Thus,

$$\ln P = \ln(12\,000\,000 \exp(0.02t)).$$

The result of using Rule 1 in Table 3.2 is

$$\ln P = \ln(12\,000\,000) + \ln(\exp(0.02t)). \tag{3.7}$$

By Rule 2a of Table 3.3,

$$\ln(\exp(0.02t)) = 0.02t,$$

and substituting into equation (3.7):

$$\ln P = \ln(12\,000\,000) + 0.02t. \tag{3.8}$$

Compare this with the general form of linear function $y = mx + c$:

$$
\begin{array}{ccccc}
y & = & mx & + & c \\
\downarrow & & \downarrow & & \downarrow \\
\ln P & = & 0.02t & + & \ln(12\,000\,000)
\end{array}
$$

If we regard $\ln P$ as equivalent to y, 0.02 as equivalent to m, t as equivalent to x, and $\ln(12\,000\,000)$ as equivalent to c, then we can identify a linear relationship between $\ln P$ and t.

Such a plot is called a *log–lin* plot.

A plot of $\ln P$ against t should result in a straight line, of slope 0.02, which crosses the $\ln P$ axis at $\ln(12\,000\,000)$. This is not particularly interesting here because we know the values 12 000 000 and 0.02 already. Suppose though that, in some general case, we want to try using the general form of exponential function

$$P = a \exp(bt) \qquad (c \le t \le d) \tag{3.9}$$

to create a continuous model for a population for which we have some data. The first thing to do is to take logarithms of both sides of (3.9):

$$\ln P = \ln(a \exp(bt)) \qquad (c \le t \le d).$$

Rule 1 from Table 3.2 then gives

$$\ln P = \ln a + \ln(\exp(bt)) \qquad (c \le t \le d).$$

But, by Rule 2a from Table 3.3, $\ln(\exp(bt)) = bt$, so this means that

$$\ln P = \ln a + bt \qquad (c \le t \le d).$$

So, given some data on population versus time, for which you suspect some version of the exponential function to be appropriate, it is a good idea to plot the natural logarithm of population against time. If the exponential function is appropriate, the resulting data points should lie on or near a straight line. The slope of the straight line will give a value for b and the intercept with the $\ln P$ axis will give a value for $\ln a$. You will have carried out a **logarithmic transformation** of the original data for P. An opportunity to try out this will arise in your computing work for this chapter.

A similar procedure will work also if the exponential function that is used to create the model is any exponential function rather than the natural exponential function. For example, suppose that we try to use the function

$$P = A \times 2^{Bt} \qquad (C \le t \le D), \tag{3.10}$$

where A and B are constant parameters to be found from some given data.

We can take natural logarithms again to convert (3.10) to

$$\ln P = \ln(A \times 2^{Bt}) \qquad (C \le t \le D).$$

Rule 1 from Table 3.2 then gives

$$\ln P = \ln A + \ln(2^{Bt}) \qquad (C \le t \le D). \tag{3.11}$$

Rule 3 from Table 3.2, applied to the term $\ln(2^{Bt})$ of (3.11), gives

$$\ln(2^{Bt}) = Bt \ln 2 = (B \ln 2)t,$$

and so (3.10) becomes

$$\ln P = \ln A + (B \ln 2)t \qquad (C \le t \le D). \tag{3.12}$$

Again we have a straight line function, with the same intercept as before but with slope $B \ln 2$.

Activity 3.3   *Linearising a particular equation*

In Section 7 of Chapter A4, the amount of money $£M$ owed after compound interest of 5% p.a. for n years was worked out as

$$M = 10\,000 \times 1.05^n.$$

Find a linearised form of this equation.

Comment

The solution is given on page 68.

The linearisation procedure also works if logarithms other than natural logarithms are used. Let us start again with equation (3.10):

$$P = A \times 2^{Bt} \qquad (C \le t \le D).$$

If we take logarithms to base 10 instead of natural logarithms and use Note 1 following Table 3.3, we get

$$\log_{10} P = \log_{10}(A \times 2^{Bt}) \qquad (C \le t \le D).$$

Rule 1 from Table 3.2 then gives

$$\log_{10} P = \log_{10} A + \log_{10}(2^{Bt}) \qquad (C \le t \le D). \tag{3.13}$$

Using Rule 3 from Table 3.2 converts (3.13) to

$$\log_{10} P = \log_{10} A + (B \log_{10} 2)t \qquad (C \le t \le D).$$

The graph of this function is a straight line again, but this time it has slope $B \log_{10} 2$.

Activity 3.4   Linearising a general equation

(a) Write down the linear function corresponding to taking logarithms to the base 10 of the general exponential function

$$P = a\exp(bt) \qquad (c \le t \le d).$$

(b) Write down the slope of the corresponding graph.

Comment

The solutions are given on page 68.

Mathcad uses 'log' to represent logarithms to the base 10.

If you are interleaving your computer work with your study of the main text, this would be a convenient point to continue work on Chapter C3, Section 5 of Computer Book C; you could now carry out Activity 5.2 in Subsection 5.2.

It is not always necessary to declare the subscript 10 when indicating logarithms to base 10. It has been done here to make the distinction from natural logarithms clearer. If you meet the abbreviation 'log' for the logarithm function elsewhere, it may imply 'to the base 10'. In the remainder of this chapter, the subscript 10 is dropped where $\log_{10}$ is implied.

3.3   Exponential decrease

Chapter C1, Section 5 considered the depreciation costs per year, £D, for a car in terms of the age A years of the car when bought. The function

$$D = 2500\exp(-0.25A) \qquad (0 \le A \le 6)$$

was considered appropriate on the grounds that:

(a) D had a fixed value of £2500 when $A = 0$,

(b) D decreased as A increased, and

(c) D decreased faster when A was small than when A was large.

A plot of this function is shown in Figure 3.3.

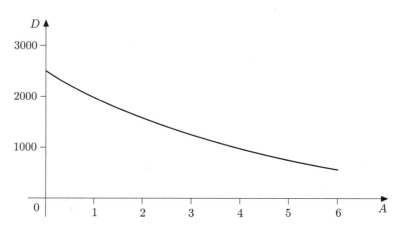

Figure 3.3

Chapter C2, Section 3 introduced a similar but more general function that could be used in a mathematical model of radioactive decay. The mass m kg of radioactive substance remaining at time t s could be expressed by

$$m = m_0\exp(-\lambda t) \qquad (t \ge 0)$$

where m_0 kg is the mass to start with and $\lambda > 0$. Note that although the dependent variable, m, becomes very small as the independent variable t

increases, it never quite becomes zero. The corresponding differential equation for rate of the change in the value of m is

$$\frac{dm}{dt} = -\lambda m.$$

So this rate depends both on the amount of radioactive mass remaining and on the value of λ, which represents the instantaneous fractional *decay rate*.

Activity 3.5   Recalling examples of exponential change

Exponential change is described by functions of the form

$$y = pq^{rx}$$

where p, q and r are constants.

(a) List examples you have met for quantities or numbers corresponding to y, x, p, q and r respectively.

(b) Do you agree that, in the majority of contexts, $p > 0$? Why is this the case?

(c) For positive p, q, r and x, how should the general expression be altered to represent a *decreasing* exponential function?

Comment

Solutions are given on page 68.

A different sort of decreasing exponential function was introduced in Chapter A4 in the context of mortgage repayments. If the mortgage is represented by g and time by t in years, then a specific example, corresponding to a £10 000 loan at a fixed rate of interest of 5% per annum being repaid over 23 years by annual instalments of £750, is

$$g = 15\,000 - 5000(1.05)^t \qquad (0 \le t \le 23). \tag{3.14}$$

Rule 4 of Table 3.3, applied to the expression $(1.05)^t$ in (3.14), gives

You saw this formula in Subsection 7.3 of Chapter A4.

$$(1.05)^t = \exp(kt) \text{ where } k = \ln(1.05).$$

This gives a value for k of 0.048 790 164 2.

As long as k is positive, the form (3.14) for g is such that an exponentially-increasing term $(5000 \exp(kt))$ is being subtracted from a constant (15 000). So we expect g to decrease at an increasing rate.

When $t = 0$,

$$g = 15\,000 - 5000 \exp 0 = 15\,000 - 5000 = 10\,000, \tag{3.15}$$

which corresponds to the initial debt of £10 000. In the context of mortgage repayments, we want to know when $g = 0$ since that represents the time at which the mortgage is repaid.

Activity 3.6   Expected values

(a) Check whether the value of k worked out above is consistent with the amount owed being paid off during the 23rd year.

(b) Start with a more general form,

$$g = A - B\exp(kt) \qquad (0 \le t \le T).$$

   (i) Find the value of g at $t = 0$.

   (ii) Find the value of k so that $g = 0$ when $t = T$.

   (iii) Sketch a graph of g against t.

Comment

The solutions are given on page 68.

Note how the slope of the curve becomes 'more negative' as t increases.

Your work for part (b) of Activity 3.6 shows the behaviour of the general form of function

$$g = A - B\exp(kt) \qquad (0 \le t \le T).$$

This function decreases at an increasing rate as t increases, but the decrease is from an initial value $(A - B)$.

3.4   Growth and decay to a limit

Example 3.1   Safe landing

In Chapter C1, Section 4, Example 4.2, a function corresponding to the velocity of a parachutist after the opening of the parachute was written as

$$v = 8 + 22\exp(-1.25t) \qquad (t \ge 0), \tag{3.16}$$

where $v\,\mathrm{m\,s}^{-1}$ is the instantaneous velocity at time $t\,\mathrm{s}$.

Let us look at some of the properties and modelling implications of this function.

Chapter C1 worked out, by differentiating, that the corresponding function for the acceleration is
$a = -27.5\exp(-1.25t)\ (t \ge 0)$
which is another example of a decaying exponential.

Consider first the value of v when $t = 0$:

$$v = 8 + 22\exp(0) = 8 + 22$$
$$= 30.$$

The function predicts that the parachutist is moving at $30\,\mathrm{m\,s}^{-1}$ when the parachute opens.

Consider next the value of v when t is arbitrarily large. For such a value of t, $\exp(-1.25t)$ would be arbitrarily small, so v would be very close to the value 8. The modelling interpretation of this is that the velocity is very close to a constant value, $8\,\mathrm{m\,s}^{-1}$, which will be maintained until the parachutist lands.

Incidentally, the steady velocity, that is approached by the parachutist (or anything else falling against air resistance), is called the *terminal* velocity. The parachute, of course, is to ensure that the terminal velocity is sufficiently low ($8\,\mathrm{m\,s}^{-1}$ in the specific case we have looked at here) to give a reasonably gentle landing and so avoid injury.

Now consider what happens as t increases from near zero. When t is near zero, the speed will be near $30\,\mathrm{m\,s^{-1}}$. The amount being added to 8 through the term $22\exp(-1.25t)$ is close to 22. As t increases, the value of $22\exp(-1.25t)$ decreases fairly rapidly at first and then more gradually until v approaches 8.

The result of this is sketched in Figure 3.4.

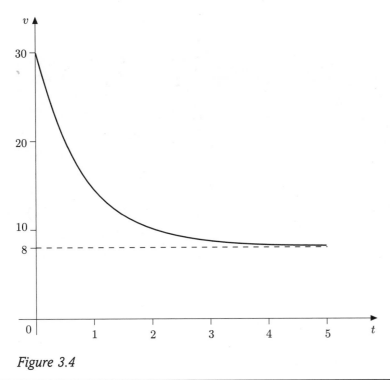

Figure 3.4

The process of gradual diminution of the parachutist's velocity towards terminal velocity is known as **decay to a limit**: decay because the velocity is initially greater than the limit and decreases. Conversely, **growth to a limit** involves a quantity which is initially below the limit and increases towards that limit.

Example 3.2   Another safe landing

If the parachutist had opened his parachute while his velocity was somewhat *below* terminal velocity, then the velocity might have been appropriately modelled by a function such as (for example):

$$v = 8 - 3\exp(-1.25t) \qquad (t \geq 0). \tag{3.17}$$

Activity 3.7   How fast was the parachutist falling?

Assuming that $t = 0$ at the instant the parachutist opened his parachute, what was his downward velocity at that instant according to equation (3.17)?

Comment

The solution is given on page 69.

In the case of equation (3.17), the term $-3\exp(-1.25t)$ represents an ever-decreasing amount that is *subtracted from* the terminal velocity 8, so that as t increases, the parachutist's velocity increases fairly rapidly at first, then more gradually until v approaches 8. The result is sketched in Figure 3.5.

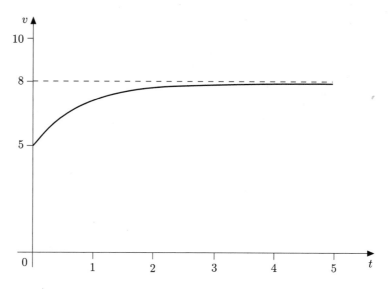

Figure 3.5

In general, assuming that the limit being approached has positive values, a growth-to-a-limit function has the form

$$y = a - b\exp(-kx) \qquad (C \le x \le D), \tag{3.18}$$

while a decay-to-a-limit function has the form

$$y = a + b\exp(-kx) \qquad (C \le x \le D), \tag{3.19}$$

where in both (3.18) and (3.19), a, b and k are positive constants (parameters) and C and D represent values of the independent variable between which the function is valid. Let us check on their properties.

Growth to a limit

In equation (3.18), when $x = 0$, $y = a - b\exp 0 = a - b$, so that in the (usual) case where x is measured from the start of the interval of validity, the parameter C is 0 and the dependent variable takes the value $a - b$ at the start of the interval.

Consider the derivative of y with respect to x. We do the differentiation term by term. Using Table 3.2 in Chapter C1, and the Constant Multiple Rule, the derivative of the constant a is zero and the derivative of $b\exp(-kx)$ is $-bk\exp(-kx)$. So

$$\frac{dy}{dx} = bk\exp(-kx).$$

As x increases, therefore, dy/dx becomes smaller, so y will increase from the value $a - b$ but at an ever decreasing rate. As $b\exp(-kx)$ becomes very small, y approaches the value a. This value represents the limit towards which y grows. If a function of this general form were being used to create a model of population growth to a limit, then a would represent the limiting population, and $a - b$ would represent the starting population.

There are three parameters, a, b, and k in the general form. Knowledge of the initial and limiting populations gives only two pieces of information. A value for the population at some non-zero time is needed also to evaluate the third parameter.

Example 3.3   Bacterial growth

Suppose we wish to find a function to describe the first six hours of growth of a food-limited bacterial culture that has 300 cells when first counted and 600 cells after 30 minutes. We are told that after a period of time which exceeds 18 hours it appears to approach a limit of around 4000 cells. We could start by assuming the general form of a growth-to-limit function for the bacteria population, with time measured in hours:

$$P = a - b \exp(-kt).$$

When $t = 0$ (at the start of counting), $P = 300$. Since the general form gives $P = a - b$ when $t = 0$, this means that

$$a - b = 300.$$

The limit of P according to the general form is a, so $a = 4000$. From this and the value of $a - b$, we have $b = 3700$. Finally we can use the information that $P = 600$ when t (measuring time in hours) $= 0.5$. Substitution in the general form gives

$$600 = 4000 - 3700 \exp(-0.5k)$$
$$3400 = 3700 \exp(-0.5k)$$
$$\frac{3400}{3700} = \exp(-0.5k)$$
$$\ln\left(\frac{34}{37}\right) = -0.5k$$
$$k = -2\ln\left(\frac{34}{37}\right) = 0.1691 \simeq 0.17.$$

Note, as a check, that k turns out to be positive as required for a growth-to-limit behaviour.

Finally the required function may be written

$$P = 4000 - 3700 \exp(-0.1691t) \qquad (0 \le t \le 6).$$

As a check we should try $t = 18$ in this equation, because we have been given the information that after 18 hours the limit seems to be 4000 cells. The result is $P = 3827$, which is reasonably close to the required value of 4000.

Activity 3.8   Finding a population growth function

(a) Find a function that could be used to model the growth of a population that has a value of 3000 when counts start and reaches a value of 6000 after 1 year. It appears to approach a limit of about 12000 after a period which exceeds 10 years.

(b) Sketch this function.

Comment

The solutions are given on page 69.

If you are interleaving your computer work with your study of the main text, this would be a convenient point to finish Subsection 5.2 of Chapter C3 in Computer Book C, by carrying out Activity 5.3.

Decay to a limit

In equation (3.19), when $x = 0$, $y = a + b \exp 0 = a + b$, so that (again in the case when x is measured from the start of the interval of validity) $C = 0$ and the dependent variable takes the value $a + b$ at the start of the interval.

Differentiating y with respect to x in (3.19), we obtain this time

$$\frac{dy}{dx} = -bk \exp(-kx).$$

As x increases, the size of dy/dx becomes smaller (though it remains negative), so y will *decrease* from the value $a + b$ but at an ever-decreasing rate, the limiting population being a as before.

Activity 3.9   Rabbit crash

Imagine that a population of rabbits on a nature reserve has been roughly stable at 5000, when a sudden ecological catastrophe makes that population level non-viable. After a month it has decreased to 3000, and two years later it seems to have settled at about 1500.

(a) Find a function to model the first year of this population decline, measuring time in months.

(b) Sketch this function.

Comment

Solutions are given on page 69.

3.5   Logarithmic functions

A branch of psychology, called experimental psychology, is concerned with observing and measuring human response to various stimuli. In particular, our sensations of light, colour, sound, taste, touch and muscular tension are produced when an external stimulus acts on the associated sense. Gustav Fechner, a German scientist of the late nineteenth century, studied the results of experiments on sensations of heat, light and sound and associated stimuli by another German called Ernst Weber. Weber measured the response of subjects, in a laboratory setting and using scales of his devising, to input stimuli measured in terms of energy or some other physical attribute and discovered that:

1   no sensation is felt until the stimulus reaches a certain value, known as the *threshold value T*;

2   after this threshold is reached, an increase in stimulus I produces an increase in sensation S;

3   this increase in sensation occurs at a diminishing rate as the stimulus is increased.

Activity 3.10 Modelling Weber's results

(a) Do Weber's results suggest a linear or non-linear relationship between sensation and stimulus? Sketch a graph of sensation S against stimulus I according to Weber's results.

(b) Consider whether an exponential function or a limit-to-growth function might be appropriate.

Comment

Solutions are given on page 69.

Fechner suggested that an appropriate function is a *logarithmic* one. He suggested that the variation in sensation (S) with stimulus input (I) is

$$S = A \log(I/T) \qquad (I \geq T) \tag{3.20}$$

where I is the independent variable, and A and T are positive parameters, T representing the threshold of stimulus input below which there is no sensation. Note that when $I = T$, $\log(I/T) = \log 1 = 0$, so this function is consistent with item 1 of Weber's results. When $I = 10T$, $S = A \log(10) = A$. When $I = 100T$, $S = A \log(100) = 2A$. The logarithmic function predicts that a tenfold increase in the stimulus input from T to $10T$ will result in the same change in sensation as a further tenfold increase in stimulus input to $100T$. Each tenfold change in stimulus results in an increase of A in sensation. So, although sensation is predicted to increase with stimulus, the stimulus has to increase at a faster and faster rate to achieve a given change in sensation. These points are consistent with items 2 and 3 of Weber's findings. Fechner's suggestion, that the logarithmic function is an appropriate one for a model of the relationship between sensation and stimulus, seems reasonable.

Note that the logarithmic function suggested by Fechner is not defined for zero stimulus, but we are in any case interested in the model only at and above the threshold stimulus, i.e. for values of the logarithm equal to and above zero. Note also that the logarithmic function is useful for looking at changes in sensation relative to stimulus values other than the threshold stimulus. According to Rule 2 in Table 3.2, Fechner's sensation function may be written

$$S = A \log(I/T) = A(\log I - \log T) \qquad (I \geq T).$$

Suppose that the sensation has the value S_1 at I_1 and S_2 at I_2, so that

$$S_1 = A(\log I_1 - \log T) \qquad (I_1 \geq T), \tag{3.21}$$

and

$$S_2 = A(\log I_2 - \log T) \qquad (I_2 \geq T). \tag{3.22}$$

If we subtract (3.21) from (3.22), we get

$$S_2 - S_1 = A(\log I_2 - \log I_1) = A \log(I_2/I_1),$$

where Rule 2 of Table 3.2 has been used again for the last step. According to this form of equation, the change in sensation between two stimulus values depends on the ratio of the stimulus values.

Another point to note is that the relationship between the variables in a logarithmic function is really the inverse of that between the variables in the exponential function.

Let us start with equation (3.20) again:

$$S = A \log(I/T) \qquad (I \geq T).$$

Divide both sides by A.

$$\frac{S}{A} = \log\left(\frac{I}{T}\right) \qquad (I \geq T). \tag{3.23}$$

Take 10 to the power of the left-hand side of (3.23), and equate it to 10 to the power of the right-hand side:

$$10^{S/A} = 10^{\log(I/T)} \qquad (I \geq T), \tag{3.24}$$

and using Rule 3b of Table 3.3 for the right-hand side of (3.24):

$$10^{S/A} = I/T \qquad (I \geq T),$$

or

$$I = T \times 10^{S/A} \qquad (I \geq T).$$

Since this is now a law relating I to S rather than S to I, we should restate the range of validity in terms of S. Clearly, I increases with S and is equal to T when $S = 0$, so our final form of the law expressed this way round is

$$I = T \times 10^{S/A} \qquad (S \geq 0).$$

This is an exponential relationship between stimulus and sensation. A logarithmic relationship between sensation and stimulus therefore implies an exponential relationship between stimulus and sensation. The relationship may be written in two different forms, with the variables playing opposite roles in the two functions.

The logarithmic relationship between sensation and stimulus is known as the *Weber–Fechner Law of Sensation*. The idea that a mathematical function could describe our sensations was quite startling when it was first propounded. Indeed it may seem quite amazing to you now. It does not always work, but, nevertheless, the idea has been quite fruitful: out of it has come much quantitative experimental psychology.

Activity 3.11   Inverting a logarithmic function

Given a relationship between y and x of the form

$$y = 3 \log(x/4) \quad (x \geq 4),$$

what is the relationship between x and y?

Comment

The solution is given on page 70.

3.6 Power law functions

An exponential function is not the only one that could be considered for modelling non-linear growth or non-linear decay. Section 2 of this chapter looked at modelling uses of quadratic functions. An example of a quadratic function that represents non-linear growth in the given range is

$$s = \frac{t^2}{9} \qquad (0 \le t \le 30). \tag{3.25}$$

This function describes jogger Mary's position along the street and has a rate of change that varies with time:

$$\frac{ds}{dt} = \frac{2t}{9} \qquad (0 \le t \le 30).$$

The function (3.25) for s can be compared with

$$s = \frac{10}{3}t \qquad (0 \le t \le 30), \tag{3.26}$$

which describes jogger Tom's position. The rate of change for function (3.26) is

$$\frac{ds}{dt} = \frac{10}{3}, \text{ a constant.}$$

The audio tape for Chapter A4 introduced some *cubic* functions. An example of such a function is

$$s = \frac{t^3}{90} \qquad (0 \le t \le 30).$$

For this case

$$\frac{ds}{dt} = \frac{t^2}{30} \qquad (0 \le t \le 30).$$

A jogger moving in a way consistent with this function for distance would begin very much more slowly than Mary, but would rapidly catch up, and at the end of 30 seconds would be running nearly five times as fast as Mary!

These quadratic and cubic functions are particular types of a **power law function**, so-called because the independent variable (t in the examples just given) is raised to some power or exponent. If there is no reason to choose a power of 2 or 3 in particular, then a more general form of a power law function exhibiting non-linear growth is

$$y = kx^n,$$

where k, n are constants.

Power law functions may be appropriate in modelling situations that involve proportionality. For example, experiments show that the drag force on an object subject to various kinds of flow is found to be proportional to the speed of flow raised to various powers, the power being dependent on the type of flow. If F represents force and v denotes speed of flow, then an appropriate function here would be

$$F = kv^n \qquad (v \ge 0),$$

where k and n are positive constants and n, called the *exponent* or *power* of x, is not necessarily a whole number.

The question arises of finding specific values of k and n appropriate to specific data.

The fact that the logarithm function turns a product into a sum comes to our aid. Let us take logarithms of $F = kv^n$.

By Note (a) immediately following Table 3.3, we can use logarithms to base 10 just the same as natural logarithms, and in practice it is often more convenient to do so.

Using Rule 1 from Table 3.2, we get

$$\log F = \log k + \log(v^n) \qquad (v \geq 0).$$

Now we use Rule 3 from Table 3.2 to get

$$\log F = \log k + n \log v \qquad (v \geq 0).$$

Compare this with the general straight-line function $y = mx+c$.

$$
\begin{array}{ccccc}
y & = & m & x & + & c \\
\downarrow & & \downarrow & \downarrow & & \downarrow \\
\log F & = & n & \log v & + & \log k
\end{array}
$$

If you consider $\log F$ equivalent to y, $\log v$ equivalent to x, n equivalent to m and $\log k$ equivalent to c, the equation with logarithms is that of a straight line.

Such a plot is called a *log–log* plot.

In other words, a plot of $\log F$ against $\log v$ produces a straight line. Measurement of the slope of this line gives a value for n, and the intercept of the line with the $\log F$ axis gives a value for $\log k$ and hence k (see Figure 3.6). The power law that we started with has been linearised by means of logarithms.

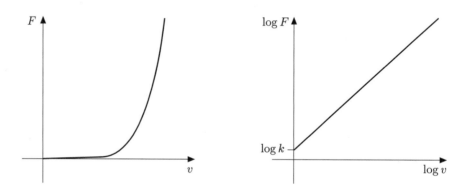

Figure 3.6

Let us try the same procedure based on taking logarithms of an equation, to linearise an example power law of the form

$$F = 2v^7 \qquad (v > 0).$$
$$\log F = \log(2v^7)$$
$$\log F = \log 2 + \log(v^7)$$
$$\log F = \log 2 + 7 \log v.$$

In this case, a graph of $\log F$ against $\log v$ should be a straight line of slope 7 cutting the $\log F$ axis at $\log 2$.

Activity 3.12   Non-uniform flow

Suppose that you are faced with the results of an experiment in which the rate of flow $f \, \mathrm{l s^{-1}}$ of liquid out of a container has been measured at various times as the level of liquid ($h \, \mathrm{cm}$) inside the container decreases from an initial level of 50 cm to a final level of 1 cm. A plot of the results (Figure 3.7) looks non-linear.

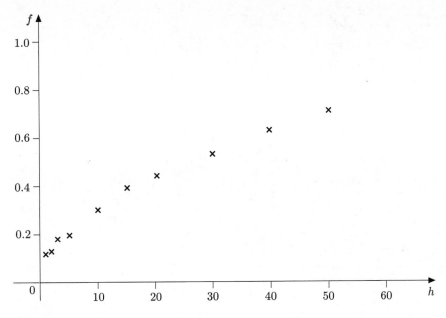

Figure 3.7

If you plot $\log f$ against $\log h$, the resulting data points seem to fit well to a straight line of slope 0.495, and the intercept on the $\log f$ axis is -1. (See Figure 3.8.)

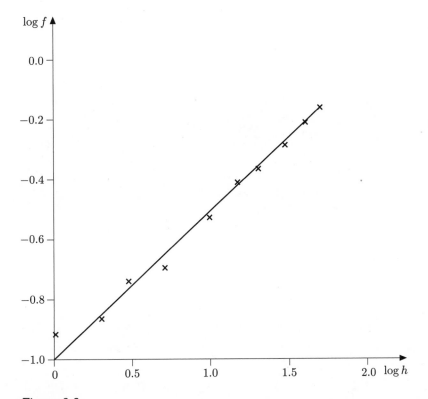

Figure 3.8

(a) Find a function to express the relationship between rate of flow and level of liquid.

(b) What rate and level correspond to the intercept on the $\log f$ axis?

Comment

Solutions are given on page 70.

Activity 3.13   Identifying difference

(a) What is the important difference between the exponents of functions corresponding to power law increase and functions corresponding to exponential increase?

(b) What is the difference between the straight-line functions resulting from the use of logarithms in either case?

(c) Identify the function types for

$$y = x^{1.2} \qquad (x > 0) \qquad \text{and} \qquad y = 1.2^x \qquad (x > 0).$$

Write down the corresponding straight-line functions.

Comment

Solutions are given on page 70.

Note that if the exponent had been $-n$ instead of n where $n > 0$, the resulting line would have a negative slope. This would correspond to an original function of the form $F = kv^{-n}$. This is a function that *decreases* non-linearly as v increases. Such a function is inappropriate in the context of drag forces since experience shows that drag usually increases with speed of flow. However, such functions may arise in other modelling contexts; contexts involving inverse proportionality, for example. In Subsection 2.3 we looked at a profit function based on a decreasing *linear* function relating demand to price for a luxury item. A linear function arises from direct proportionality. However, if we assume that demand is inversely proportional to price, this will again result in demand decreasing as price increases, but the decrease will be *non-linear*. Using Q for demand, £P for price, and k for the constant of proportionality, the corresponding function may be written

This can also be written as $Q = kP^{-1}$ $(P > 0)$.

$$Q = \frac{k}{P} \qquad (P > 0).$$

The range of validity requires that price is positive since negative price has no meaning, but note the exclusion of $P = 0$. As P approaches zero, Q increases without limit. The same is true for all functions of the form $Q = kP^{-n}$ where $n > 0$. Such functions are useful for modelling non-linear decrease only if the values of the variable that is raised to the negative power do not approach zero.

Activity 3.14   Exploring negative powers

(a) Sketch the graphical form of $y = 3x^{-2}$ for $x > 0$ and for $x < 0$.

(b) Check that the addition of a constant as in

$$y = 3 + 3x^{-2}$$

does not make this power law any more useful for modelling non-linear decreases near $x = 0$.

Comment

The solutions are given on page 70.

Activity 3.15   Summarising Section 3

A suggested form for the next few rows of the summary table is shown below. These rows are not complete. You should try to complete these rows as part of this activity. The final complete version of the table will be part of your own summary of the chapter. Feel free to alter the contents to suit what is most helpful for you. You may prefer to use different symbols from the ones given, or you may wish to add examples of other modelling contexts or, indeed, to cite different ones from those listed.

You may wish to add to your comments for Activity 2.9.

Table 3.4

Behaviour	Formula for function	Attributes	Sketch of function	Some modelling contexts
Exponential increase	$y = a \exp(bx)$ for $b > 0$	At $x = 0$, $y = a$ $\frac{dy}{dx} = by$		Population during a period of unlimited growth.
Exponential decrease	$y = a \exp(-bx)$ for $b > 0$	At $x = 0$, $y = a$ $\frac{dy}{dx} = -by$		Radioactive decay.
Growth to a limit	$y = a - b \exp(-kx)$ for $C \leq x \leq D$, $a > 0$, $b > 0$, $k > 0$	Limit is $y = a$		Population growth to a limit.
Decay to a limit				
Logarithmic increase	$y = a \log(x/A)$, $x \geq A > 0$			Weber–Fechner law of sensation.
Power law increase				Variation of position with time resulting from motion under constant acceleration.
Power law decrease				Non-linear variation of demand with price.

Summary of Section 3

◇ Exponential functions are useful for modelling non-linear increase or decrease from an initial value. They appear also in functions that are appropriate for modelling growth or decay to a limit. The appropriateness of an exponential function in describing data can be tested by a graph of the logarithm (to any base) of the dependent variable against the independent variable. If the resulting points lie on or near a straight line, then the use of an exponential function is appropriate.

◇ Logarithmic functions have been used in modelling the relationship between sensation and stimulus. More generally logarithmic functions may be used for modelling unlimited growth in which the rate of growth decreases as the independent variable increases. The logarithmic function is the inverse of the exponential function. These functions are two ways of expressing an exponential relationship between variables.

◇ Power law functions, of which certain quadratic and cubic functions are particular examples, may be used in modelling non-linear increase or decrease. The appropriateness of a power law function in describing data can be tested by a graph of the logarithm of one variable against the logarithm of the other variable. If the resulting points lie on or near a straight line, then the use of a power law function is appropriate.

Exercises for Section 3

Exercise 3.1

After administration of a drug, which enters the blood stream instantaneously, the instantaneous fractional decay rate of the concentration of the drug in the bloodstream is 0.04, when time is measured in days.

(a) If the initial concentration is $0.5 \, \mathrm{mg\,l^{-1}}$, write down an exponential function for the concentration $C \, \mathrm{mg\,l^{-1}}$ as a function of time t days.

(b) What would be the concentration after 2.5 days according to this model?

Exercise 3.2

Think about the function

$$Q(t) = A\left(1 - \exp(-Bt)\right) \quad (t \geq 0)$$

where Q and t are variables and A and B are positive constants.

(a) What is the value of the function when $t = 0$?

(b) What is the value of the function when t is indefinitely large?

(c) Write down an expression for the rate of change of $Q(t)$ with t.

(d) What kind of behaviour would be modelled by the function $Q(t)$?

Exercise 3.3

The variables x and y are related in such a way that the graph of $\ln y$ against x is a straight line passing through the points $x = 1, \ln y = \frac{1}{2}$ and $x = 3, \ln y = 2$. Find the relation between x and y in the form $y = f(x)$, where f is a function to be determined.

Exercise 3.4

It is suspected that the variables x and y are related by an equation of the form

$$y = k \times 2^x$$

for some value of k. If appropriate data pairs (x_i, y_i) were available, how would you test whether this were so, and how could the value of k be determined?

4 Oscillating functions

4.1 Amplitude, period and frequency

Sine and cosine functions are possible choices when modelling behaviour that involves oscillation or motion in a circle. The usefulness of these functions is rather limited if we confine our attention to only $y = \sin x$ and $y = \cos x$. Equal acquaintance with functions such as $y = 3\sin(2x)$, $y = 5\cos(3x)$, $y = 1.3 + 2\sin(\pi x + 1)$, and so on, and other functions made up of sums of functions of this type, enables the modelling of a great variety of situations where the quantity being modelled is known to change in a periodic way.

In this subsection we shall revise these ideas by examining the behaviour of more sine and cosine functions, considering a modelling context where choice of a sine function is appropriate.

Sine and cosine functions were discussed in the audiotape for Chapter A4 (Audiotape 1, Band 4), and the concepts of *amplitude* and *frequency* introduced. Consider, for example, the four functions whose graphs are shown in Figure 4.1:

$$y = \cos x, \ y = 3\sin(2x), \ y = 5\cos(3x), \ y = 1.3 + 2\sin(\pi x + 1).$$

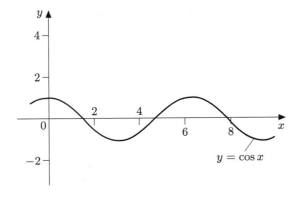

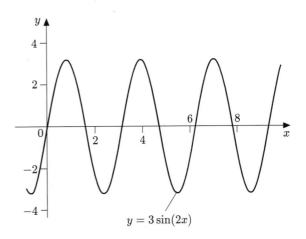

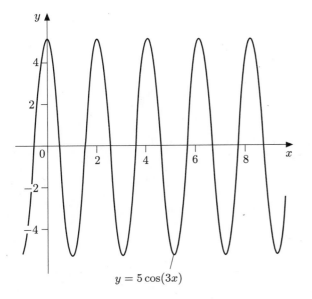

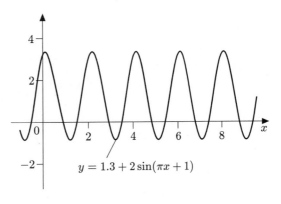

Figure 4.1

Not only are these functions oscillating functions, like $y = \sin x$, they all oscillate in essentially the same way as $y = \sin x$; the peaks and troughs occur smoothly and at equal intervals. In fact, each of these graphs can be obtained by taking the graph of $y = \sin x$ and moving it up, down, right or left (or a combination of these), combined with stretching or compressing along the x-direction or the y-direction or both. Any function that can be obtained from $y = \sin x$ in this way is called a **sinusoidal function**, and has the general form

$$y = a + b\sin(kx + c)$$

where a, b, c and k are the **parameters** of the function.

The **amplitude** of a sinusoidal function is the difference between the maximum value which it attains and its mean value, see Figure 4.2. (Alternatively, it is the difference between the mean value and the minimum value, or half the difference between the maximum and minimum values.)

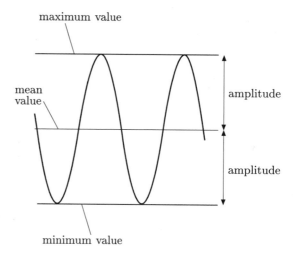

Figure 4.2

For example, the mean value of $y = \sin x$ is 0, while its maximum value is 1 (attained when $x = \dfrac{\pi}{2}, \dfrac{5\pi}{2}, \ldots$) and its minimum value is -1 (attained when $x = \dfrac{3\pi}{2}, \dfrac{7\pi}{2}, \ldots$). Thus its amplitude is $1 - 0$ or $0 - (-1)$ or $\frac{1}{2}(1 - (-1)) = 1$. For the function $y = 1.3 + 2\sin(\pi x + 1)$ the mean value is 1.3 and the maximum and minimum are $1.3 + 2 = 3.3$ and $1.3 - 2 = -0.7$ respectively, with amplitude $(1.3 + 2) - 1.3 = 2$.

Activity 4.1   Amplitudes

Find the amplitudes of the sinusoidal functions:

(a) $y = \cos x$,   (b) $y = 3\sin(2x)$,   (c) $y = 3\sin(2x + 1)$,

(d) $y = 3 - 4\sin(2x)$,   (e) $y = \sqrt{2}\sin(\pi x)$.

Comment

The solutions are given on page 71.

For a sinusoidal function of the general form

$$y = a + b\sin(kx + c),$$

the amplitude is $|b|$.

Before defining the frequency of a sinusoidal function, let us look at the closely related concept of *period*. The **period** of an oscillating function is the change in the value of x during one complete cycle of y-values (or more generally, the change in the value of the independent variable during a complete cycle of values of the dependent variable), see Figure 4.3.

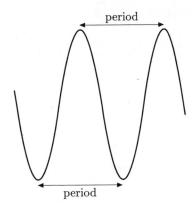

Figure 4.3

Now a complete cycle of values of $y = \sin x$ requires a change in x of 2π: from 0 to π, $\sin x$ rises then falls back to 0, while from π to 2π, it becomes negative then rises back to 0, ready to start the cycle again. Thus the period of $y = \sin x$ is 2π.

Activity 4.2   Periods

Find the periods of the sinusoidal functions:

(a) $y = \cos x$,   (b) $y = 3\sin(2x)$,   (c) $y = 3\sin(2x + 1)$,

(d) $y = 3 - 4\sin(2x)$,   (e) $y = \sqrt{2}\sin(\pi x)$.

Comment

The solutions are given on page 71.

The **frequency** of a sinusoidal function is the number of complete cycles of y-values in each advance by 1 in the value of x (or more generally, the number of complete cycles in the dependent variable in each advance by 1 in the value of the independent variable). Thus, for example, since an advance by 1 in the value of x (say from 0 to 1) takes us only $\dfrac{1}{2\pi}$ of the way through one cycle of $y = \sin x$, the frequency of this function is $\dfrac{1}{2\pi}$.

Activity 4.3   Frequencies

Find the frequencies of the sinusoidal functions:

(a) $y = \cos x$,   (b) $y = 3\sin(2x)$,   (c) $y = 3\sin(2x + 1)$,

(d) $y = 3 - 4\sin(2x)$,   (e) $y = \sqrt{2}\sin(\pi x)$.

Comment

The solutions are given on page 71.

There is thus a very straightforward connection between period and frequency: each is the reciprocal of the other, or

period × frequency = 1.

These quantities can easily be calculated for a function of the general form

$$y = a + b\sin(kx + c);$$

the frequency is $\dfrac{k}{2\pi}$ and the period is $\dfrac{2\pi}{k}$.

4.2 Modelling tides

Chapter A2 (Section 7.1) suggested that the function

$$h = 3.2\sin(2.7t + 8.5)$$

might be used to model the rise and fall of the tide in a harbour.

Figure 4.4 shows a graph of this function for $(0 \le t \le 5)$.

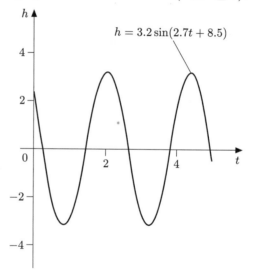

Figure 4.4

Let us consider some aspects of this graph and model. Although no units were specified in Chapter A2, it seems reasonable to suppose that the tide creates an oscillation of the water level in the harbour of h m about some mean value represented on the graph by $h = 0$. There seems to be a low tide near $t = 1$ and another after $t = 3$. Since we expect intervals of 12 to 14 hours between low tides around the UK, this suggests that time is specified in 6-hour intervals.

Activity 4.4   A tide function

Write down the amplitude, period and frequency of the function.

Comment

The solution is given on page 71.

The peak levels of the graph correspond to times when the sine function has the value 1. The lowest points correspond to times when the sine function is -1.

So far all of this may be deduced from the values $b = 3.2$ and $k = 2.7$ in the general form $y = a + b\sin(kx)$, and from the modelling context. However, there is an additional term in the function being considered here. This is a constant $c = 8.5$ within the specification of the independent variable in the sine function. When $t = 0$ the presence of this constant means that the intercept on the height axis is $3.2\sin(8.5) = 2.56$, implying that the water level is $2.56\,\text{m}$ above the mean value at the start of timing. If the constant had been zero, the graph would have passed through $(0,0)$. The non-zero positive constant has effectively displaced the sine curve to the left. It is known as the **phase** of the function.

As remarked earlier, at $t = 0$, this function has the value $3.2\sin(8.5)$. Since $\sin(8.5) = \sin(8.5 - 2\pi) = \sin(2.2168)$, we can replace the constant 8.5 by 2.2168 without altering the values on the graph. The shift by a whole cycle (a change of 2π in phase) has no effect on the graph. This means that the function

Phase is measured in radians as it is an angle.

$$h = 3.2\sin(2.7t + 2.2168)$$

does just as well as the original function in representing the tidal variation in the harbour. Let us rewrite this latest form of the function, representing the variation of water level in the harbour, so that time is measured in hours rather than in six-hourly intervals. The effect of changing the units of time from six-hour units to one-hour units is to decrease the coefficient of t in the sine function by a factor of 6, so that the new function is

$$h = 3.2\sin(0.45t + 2.2168)$$

(see Figure 4.5).

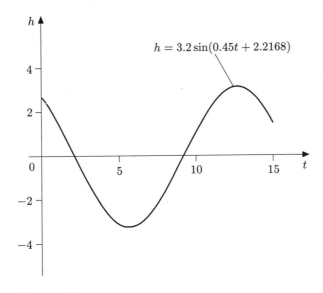

Figure 4.5

We can use the latest form of the function to calculate the time of the first low tide assuming that $t = 0$ corresponds to midnight. At the first low tide, $h = -3.2$ and

$$\sin(0.45t + 2.2168) = -1,$$
$$\text{or} \quad (0.45t + 2.2168) = 3\pi/2,$$
$$0.45t = 3\pi/2 - 2.2168 = 2.4956,$$
$$t = 5.5458.$$

So the first low tide is a little after 5.30 am.

Activity 4.5   Tide times

Assume that $t = 0$ corresponds to midnight. Calculate

If you are interleaving your computer work with your study of the main text, this would be a convenient point to work through Subsection 5.3 of Chapter C3 in Computer Book C.

(a) the time of the first high tide after midnight,

(b) the times either side of midnight at which the water level is at the mean level.

Comment

The solutions are given on page 71.

Activity 4.6   The general sinusoidal function

Summarise, in your own words, the meaning and influence of the parameters a, b, c and k in the general form of sinusoidal (i.e. oscillating) function

$$y = a + b\sin(kx + c) \qquad (x \geq 0).$$

Your summary should contain reference to amplitude, period, phase and mean value.

Activity 4.7   Modelling water level in a harbour

TV16 *Refining the View* features a 'breathing lake' whose level is a sinusoidal function.

Write down a function relating water level ($L\,$m) in a harbour to time (t hours), starting when the level is equal to the mean level of $5\,$m, that has an amplitude of $2\,$m and a period of twelve hours.

Comment

The solution is given on page 71.

Activity 4.8   Summarising Section 4

Table 4.1 suggests some final entries for the chapter summary table. Parts of it have been left incomplete deliberately for you to complete or edit. Make additional entries based on your current understanding and specifically look for modelling situations mentioned earlier in the course that can be added to the final column. Make notes first in your Learning File before transferring suitably abbreviated examples to the table.

Table 4.1   Behaviour types and corresponding functions

Behaviour	Formula for function	Attributes	Sketch of function	Modelling examples
Oscillatory	$y = a + b\sin(kx + c)$ a, b, c and k are constants	$y = a + b\sin c$ at $x = 0$ mean value is a period $= 2\pi/k$ amplitude $= |b|$		Level of tidal water

Summary of Section 4

◇   Placing a multiplier before $\sin x$ or $\cos x$ changes the amplitude without changing the period.

◇   Placing a multiplier before x in $\sin x$ or $\cos x$, i.e. *inside* a sine or cosine function, changes the period without changing the amplitude. Note that since period $\times$ frequency $= 1$ when one changes the other must also change.

◇   As with any function, the addition of a constant raises or lowers the whole graph of the sine or cosine function. It alters the mean value without changing the amplitude.

◇   Placing a constant or altering the constant c in $\sin(kx + c)$ or $\cos(kx + c)$ changes the phase and shifts the sine or cosine function along the x-axis.

◇   In general, the sinusoidal function $y = a + b\sin(kx + c)$ has mean value a, amplitude $|b|$, phase c, period $2\pi/k$ and frequency $k/2\pi$.

Exercises for Section 4

Exercise 4.1

A function for the variation of speed of an object, $v\,\mathrm{m\,s^{-1}}$, with time, $t\,\mathrm{s}$ is

$$v = \frac{1}{20}\sin\left(\frac{\pi t}{40}\right) \quad (0 \le t \le 40).$$

(a) What kind of behaviour is implied by this function?

(b) What is the maximum value of v?

(c) At which values of t is $v = 0$?

Exercise 4.2

The average number of hours of sunshine at a European holiday resort varies between 5 hours per day in the middle of winter and 10 hours per day in the middle of summer. A possible model for the variation in the number of hours of sunshine per day N with time of the year t days from the middle of winter is

$$N(t) = a - b\cos(kt).$$

(a) Sketch this function, marking the given values of N at corresponding values of t on your sketch, and explain why it might be appropriate.

(b) Calculate values of a, b and k from the information given.

(c) Predict the number of hours of sunshine per day 8 months after the middle of winter.

(d) State any assumptions that you have made.

Exercise 4.3

The vertical position y (expressed in metres) of a needle on a sewing machine, when it is working at a particular speed, is described by the formula

$$y = 0.001\sin(30t), \text{ where } t \text{ is measured in seconds.}$$

(a) What is the amplitude and the period of the needle's motion?

(b) At a different speed, the amplitude of the needle's movement is the same, but the period is 0.125 seconds. What is the formula for y, the needle's position?

5 Using Mathcad in modelling

The work for this chapter follows up some of the classes of functions discussed in Sections 2–4. To study this section you will need access to your computer, together with the disk with Mathcad files for Block C, and Computer Book C.

5.1 Quadratic functions

This subsection is based on the falling rock model in Section 2 of this chapter.

Refer to Computer Book C for the work in this subsection.

5.2 Exponential and logarithmic functions

This subsection introduces you to Mathcad's facility for creating log–lin and log–log plots to linearise exponential and logarithmic functions, and enables you to experiment with changing the parameters in the general expression modelling growth and decay to a limit.

Refer to Computer Book C for the work in this subsection.

5.3 Oscillating functions

This subsection enables you to experiment with changing the parameters in the general expression for a sinusoidal (i.e. oscillating) function.

Refer to Computer Book C for the work in this subsection.

Summary of Section 5

The activities in this section have explored some of Mathcad's plotting facilities and the role of parameters in various functions relating to maxima, exponential growth and decay and oscillation.

After working through them, you should be able to

◇   use the Zoom facility, in a given Mathcad graph

◇   change linear axis scales to logarithmic ones, in a given Mathcad graph

◇   explain the role of the constant parameters in

$$y = a - b\exp(-kx) \quad (x \geq 0),$$
$$y = a + b\sin(kx + c) \quad (x \geq 0).$$

As a result of the working through this chapter, you should be familiar with a menu of continuous *functions* that might be used when modelling. We have looked at constant functions, linear functions, non-linear functions including quadratic functions and power laws, functions that grow indefinitely or that grow or decay to a limit, and functions that oscillate. We have looked at general forms for these functions and the *parameters* that specify them. We have also looked at *methods* of finding values for the parameters in a given context, using simultaneous equations corresponding to points on a line, using the vertex of quadratic functions, using log–lin transformations for exponential functions, using log–log transformation for power law functions, using limits for growth or decay, and using values for amplitude, initial value and period for oscillating functions.

These functions and methods provide a tool kit for your future mathematical modelling, or more specifically, for Steps 2 and 3 of the modelling cycle.

The table resulting from your summarising activities in this chapter provides a summary of functions, parameters, behaviours, sketches and related modelling situations.

The following activities are intended to give you practice in thinking about the modelling cycle and in using the table.

Activity 6.1   Stages of modelling

At which stage or stages in the modelling cycle do you need to identify which function to use?

What is involved in the fifth step of the modelling cycle? What would you evaluate and how would you go about it? What is the purpose of this step in the cycle?

Comment

Some comments are given on page 71.

Activity 6.2   Reviewing the chapter

Choose at least one function that might be helpful in setting up particular mathematical models of the following situations and specify as much about this function (or these functions) as possible from the data given.

(a) Rain falls over a period of 20 minutes, the rainfall decreasing steadily in intensity until stopping. Denote the rate of rainfall by R cm per minute, time since the start of rainfall by t minutes and the initial intensity by S cm per minute. Find a function to describe the relationship between R and t.

(b) The rate of arrival of potential customers at a jumble sale which is to be open for four hours is expected to be greatest immediately the sale starts and to decrease to zero at the end of the sale. The rate of arrival of customers is denoted by Q people per hour, time since the start of the sale by t hours, and the maximum value of Q is 500. Find

assume quadratic function has vertex at time $t = 0$

a function that would represent a quadratic decrease in the rate of arrival of customers.

(c) During a particular season the air temperature just above the ground varies in a periodic manner over a 24-hour cycle. Find a function that would describe the air temperature over a given 24 hours. Denote air temperature by T, its maximum value during the 24 hours of interest by A, its minimum value by B and time *since the coldest moment* by t hours.

Comment

The solutions are given on page 72.

Activity 6.3   Reviewing the block

Before leaving the chapter and the block, pause to reflect on what you have achieved in studying it.

One way you could do this is by looking back at the list of learning outcomes at the end of each chapter and trying to assess how well you have achieved them. You could select one or two and ask yourself: 'How could I show how far I have achieved this outcome?' There may be evidence in the notes you have made. Your responses to the TMA questions for the block may also demonstrate your understanding.

Learning outcomes

You have been working towards the following learning outcomes.

Terms to know and use

Linear, quadratic, exponential, logarithmic, sinusoidal, initial value, limit (as in growth or decay to a limit), parameters, log–lin, log–log, power law, amplitude, period, frequency and phase.

Terms to recognise and be aware of

Vertex, appropriate function, general form, behaviour of a function, demand, supply, Weber–Fechner Law of Sensation.

Modelling skills

◇ Identifying the description of a behaviour and translating this, or an expected behaviour, into the behaviour of a function.

◇ Finding an appropriate function by identifying the relevant general form from expected or described behaviour.

Mathematical skills

Evaluating the parameters and range of validity and appropriateness of a function from information in a context description, including use of log–lin and log–log forms or graphs.

In particular,

◇ finding the gradient of a straight line from data

◇ finding the equation of a straight line from two pairs of coordinates

◇ finding the equation of a parabola from data

◇ finding the parameters of an exponential function from data

◇ finding the parameters of a growth or decay to a limit function from data

◇ finding the parameters of an oscillating function from data.

Mathcad skills

◇ Select and use the Zoom and change the plotting limits on the axes, in a given Mathcad graph.

◇ Change linear axis scales to logarithmic ones, in a given Mathcad graph.

Solutions to Activities

Solution 1.1

(a) $r = 3$ $(0 \leq t \leq 10)$.

(b)

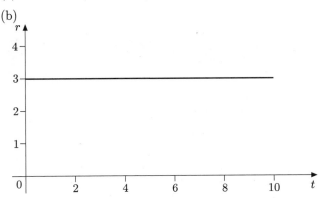

Figure S.1

(c) $\dfrac{dr}{dt} = 0$ $(0 \leq t \leq 10)$.

(d) $v = rt$ $(0 \leq t \leq 10)$.

(e) The tap will have run for seven minutes;
3 litres per minute × 7 minutes = 21 litres, or,
more generally, $7r$ litres.

Solution 1.2

(a) $a = 10$ $(0 \leq t \leq 60)$.

(b) $\dfrac{dv}{dt} = 10$ $(0 \leq t \leq 60)$.

(c) $v = \displaystyle\int \dfrac{dv}{dt}\, dt = \int 10 \, dt = 10t + c.$

The object starts from rest, so $v = 0$ when $t = 0$
and, hence, $c = 0$ and

$$v = 10t \quad (0 \leq t \leq 60).$$

(d) $s = \displaystyle\int \dfrac{ds}{dt}\, dt = \int v \, dt = \int 10t \, dt = 5t^2 + c;$

$s = 0$ when $t = 0$, so $c = 0$ and

$$s = 5t^2 \quad (0 \leq t \leq 60).$$

(e) The function is a quadratic function.

Solution 1.3

One important result of assuming that the rate of
change of a quantity is constant is that the quantity
itself varies linearly. The assumption of constant
acceleration implies a linear variation of velocity with
time and a quadratic variation of position with time.

Solution 1.4

Chapter A1 introduced linear sequences for modelling
new moon times and for the amount of tape left on a
cassette spool. Chapter B2 used a linear sequence in
the first model for the used car problem and in a
model for proportionate growth in a population of
beetles. In Chapter A4, a linear function was found
to be useful when modelling the area of a 1 m wide
border for a square garden of side x m.

Solution 1.5

(a) T_1 will be less than 2.7, since the rock will be
moving faster throughout its descent.

(b)

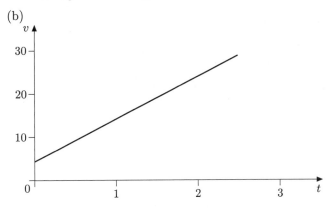

Figure S.2

The graph is still a straight line, but is displaced
upwards compared with Figure 1.4.

Solution 1.6

(a)

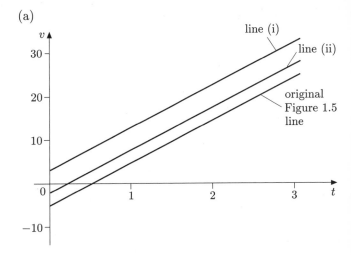

Figure S.3

(b) The effect of changing initial velocity in size or
in sign is simply to displace the straight line
upwards or downwards without changing its
slope.

(c) $v = \dfrac{9.8}{6}t \simeq 1.6t.$

(d)   The graph of velocity against time is still linear, but the change in the acceleration due to gravity changes the slope.

Solution 1.8

(a) $v = -5 + 10t \qquad (0 \le t \le 5).$

(b)

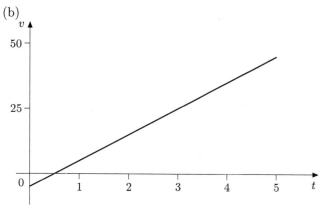

Figure S.4

(c) $-5 + 10t = 0$ when $t = 0.5$, so the upward velocity of the satellite is zero after half a second of boost.

Solution 1.9

(a)   In this answer, h cm is used for the level of water measured from the bottom of the barrel and t minutes for time. See Figure S.5.

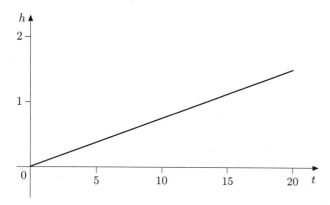

Figure S.5

(b)   The intensity of rainfall is stated to be constant, so the rate at which the barrel fills may be taken as constant. The gradient of an appropriate linear function relating level of water (h cm) measured from the bottom of the vessel and time (t minutes) would be $\frac{1.5}{20} = 0.075$, and an appropriate linear function would be

$$h = 0.075t + c.$$

Since the barrel is empty to start with, $h = 0$ when $t = 0$, implying that $c = 0$. So the

appropriate linear function and its range of validity are expressed by

$$h = 0.075t \qquad (0 \le t \le 20).$$

(c)   It is assumed that the barrel has a uniform circular cross-section, that no water is removed during the rainfall and there are no holes or leaks up to 1.5 cm depth.

(d) $h = 0.075t + 2 \qquad (0 \le t \le 20).$

Solution 1.10

For the (time, velocity) coordinates $(0, 0)$ and $(4, 15)$,

$$0 = 0m + c$$
$$15 = 4m + c.$$

From the first of these $c = 0$, and hence, in the second, $m = 3.75$.

So the acceleration up to $15 \, \mathrm{m\,s^{-1}}$ is $3.75 \, \mathrm{m\,s^{-2}}$.

For the (time, velocity) coordinates $(9, 27)$ and $(12, 30)$,

$$27 = 9m + c$$
$$30 = 12m + c.$$

Subtracting the first from the second gives

$$3 = 3m \text{ or } m = 1,$$

so the acceleration between $27 \, \mathrm{m\,s^{-1}}$ and $30 \, \mathrm{m\,s^{-1}}$ is $1 \, \mathrm{m\,s^{-2}}$.

Solution 1.11

The linear function will be of the form

$$Q = mP + c \qquad (600 \le P \le 1000).$$

The limits on P represent the given range of data on price.

Substituting the first pair of values of Q and P,

$$100\,000 = 1000m + c. \qquad (\text{S.1})$$

Substituting the second pair of values,

$$200\,000 = 600m + c. \qquad (\text{S.2})$$

Subtracting (S.1) from (S.2),

$$100\,000 = -400m$$
$$m = -250.$$

Note that the negative gradient is consistent with the fact that demand falls as price increases.

Check that the 'change in variable' definition for finding m works.
Change in dependent variable
$(Q) = 200\,000 - 100\,000 = 100\,000.$
Corresponding change in independent variable
$(P) = 600 - 1000 = -400.$
The ratio of these changes $\dfrac{100\,000}{-400} = -250.$

This value of m may be used with the first pair of values,

$$100\,000 = -250\,000 + c,$$

so $c = 350\,000$

and the linear function relating demand and price is

$$Q = 350\,000 - 250P.$$

[A *precautionary check* is to make sure that this result is consistent with the other pair of values.

When $P = 600$,

$$Q = 350\,000 - 250 \times 600 = 350\,000 - 150\,000$$
$$= 200\,000, \text{ as required.}]$$

When $P = 750$,

$$Q = 350\,000 - 250 \times 750 = 350\,000 - 187\,500$$
$$= 162\,500.$$

So a linear relationship between demand and price for this luxury suggests a demand of 162 500 items per year when the price per item is £750.

At a price of £500, $P = 500$, and the model predicts that

$$Q = -250 \times 500 + 350\,000 = 225\,000.$$

So the linear model suggests a demand of 225 000 items per year when the price per item is £500. Such a price however is outside the range of given data. Consequently the corresponding demand prediction represents an extrapolation which may not be reliable. On the other hand, the price of £750 lies within the given range of data and the corresponding demand prediction is an interpolation. If the given data points are close to each other, then interpolation between these points is regarded as more reliable than extrapolation to points further away.

Solution 2.2

(a) s corresponds to y, and t corresponds to x.

(b) $C = 0$, $A = \frac{1}{9}$ and $B = 0$.

Solution 2.3

(a) Function (2.2) is quadratic.

(b) $t = T$ when $s = 35 - 2 = 33$.

$$33 = 4.9T^2, \text{ so } T = \sqrt{\frac{33}{4.9}} \simeq 2.595.$$

(c)

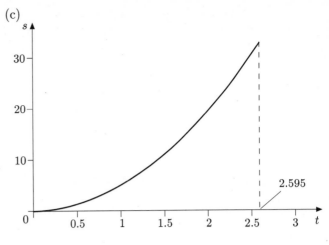

Figure S.6

Solution 2.4

(a) Here h corresponds to y and t to x in the general form. The coefficient corresponding to a is -4.9, $b = 0$ and $c = 35$. The value of a is negative so the parabola opens downwards.

(b) $h = 33 - 4.9t^2$ $(0 \le t \le 2.595)$.

(c)

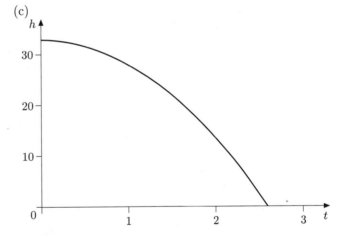

Figure S.7

Solution 2.5

(a) In Subsection 1.2, the value of t at which the rock's velocity is zero was worked out as $t = \dfrac{5}{9.8}$. This value can be used in the function for s to give

$$s = \frac{5}{9.8}\left(4.9 \times \frac{5}{9.8} - 5\right) = -\frac{25}{19.6} = -1.275\,510\,2.$$

So the rock rises to a little less than 1.28 m above the cliff-top.

(b) If position is measured as height above the ground, then the appropriate velocity function, expressed as rate of change of height (h) above the ground is

$$\frac{dh}{dt} = 5 - 9.8t \qquad (0 < t \le T).$$

67

Direct integration using standard integrals results in

$$h = 5t - 4.9t^2 + c \qquad (0 < t \leq T).$$

When $t = 0$, $h = 35$, so substituting these values in the equation for h gives $c = 35$ and the function is

$$h = 5t - 4.9t^2 + 35 \qquad (0 < t \leq T).$$

Solution 2.8

Use the general form, with $B = 0$ and $C = 2$,

$$y - 2 = A(x - 0)^2$$

or $\quad y - 2 = Ax^2$.

Then use the point $(4, 4)$, which means that $y = 4$ when $x = 4$:

$$4 - 2 = 16A$$

so $\quad A = \frac{2}{16} = \frac{1}{8}$

and the required equation is

$$y = 2 + \frac{x^2}{8}.$$

Solution 3.2

(a) At $t = 0$, $P = 12\,000\,000$, which represents the initial population. (Recall that $\exp 0 = 1$.)

(b) $\dfrac{dP}{dt} = 12\,000\,000 \times 0.01 \exp(0.01t)$. The rate of growth is controlled by the coefficient of t, which is 0.01.

(c) The time interval during which the model is valid is stated as $(0 \leq t \leq 10)$.

(d) Since for $t > 0$, $\exp(0.01t) > 1$, this implies that $P > 12\,000\,000$. As t increases towards 10, P becomes larger.

Solution 3.3

Take natural logarithms of both sides:

$$\begin{aligned} \ln M &= \ln(10\,000 \times 1.05^n) \\ &= \ln(10\,000) + \ln(1.05^n) \\ &\quad \text{(by Rule 1 of Table 3.2)} \\ &= \ln(10\,000) + n\ln(1.05) \\ &\quad \text{(by Rule 3 of Table 3.2).} \end{aligned}$$

So a plot of $\ln M$ against n would be a straight line passing through $(0, \ln(10\,000))$ with slope $\ln(1.05)$.

Solution 3.4

(a) Recalling that $\exp(bt)$ means e^{bt}:

$$\begin{aligned} \log_{10} P &= \log_{10}(ae^{bt}) \qquad (c \leq t \leq d) \\ &= \log_{10} a + \log_{10}(e^{bt}) \\ &\quad \text{(by Rule 1 of Table 3.2)} \\ &= \log_{10} a + bt \log_{10} e \\ &\quad \text{(by Rule 3 of Table 3.2)} \\ &= \log_{10} a + (b \log_{10} e)t \qquad (c \leq t \leq d). \end{aligned}$$

(b) The slope of the graph is $b \log_{10} e$.

Solution 3.5

(a) y has corresponded to population (P), depreciation costs $(£D)$ and mass m kg of radioactive substance remaining; x has been time $(t\,\text{s})$ or age $(A$ years$)$; p has corresponded to initial population (P_0), $12\,000\,000$, 2500 (for depreciation costs), and initial mass $(m_0$ kg$)$; q has been e (most frequently) and 2; r has been 0.01, 0.02, B, -0.25, and $-\lambda$.

(b) In the modelling contexts encountered so far, $p > 0$ has been appropriate since y stands for quantities which cannot be negative, such as populations, money or levels of radioactivity.

(c) If p, q, r and x are positive, then

$$y = pq^{-rx}$$

corresponds to a decreasing exponential function.

Solution 3.6

(a) When $t = 23$,

$$\begin{aligned} 15\,000 - 5000 \exp(23k) &= 15\,000 - 5000 \exp(23 \times 0.048\,790 \\ &= 15\,000 - 15\,357.62 \\ &= -357.62. \end{aligned}$$

This means that at the end of the 23rd year there would have been an overpayment of £357.62.

A similar calculation with $t = 22$ produces a positive amount owing of just over £373. This is consistent with the amount owing becoming zero some time during the 23rd year.

(b) (i) When $t = 0$, $g = A - B \exp 0 = A - B$.

(ii) When $t = T$, $g = 0$,

So $0 = A - B \exp(kT)$,

$$\exp(kT) = \frac{A}{B},$$

$$k = \frac{1}{T} \ln\left(\frac{A}{B}\right).$$

(iii)

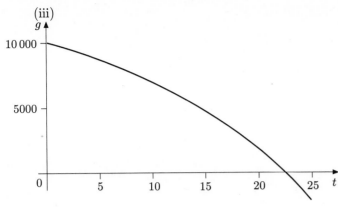

Figure S.8

Solution 3.7

Since $\exp 0 = 1$, the parachutist's downward velocity at $t = 0$ is $v = 8 - 3 \times 1 = 5 \, \text{m s}^{-1}$.

Solution 3.8

(a) Start with

$$P = a - b \exp(-kt) \qquad (0 \leq t \leq 10),$$

where P is the number of members in the population at time t years.

The given data suggest that a is 12 000 and that $a - b = 3000$.

So $b = a - 3000 = 12\,000 - 3000 = 9000$.

The corresponding curve must pass through $(1, 6000)$ so

$$6000 = 12\,000 - 9000 \exp(-k)$$
$$\exp(-k) = \frac{12\,000 - 6000}{9000} = \frac{2}{3}$$
$$-k = \ln(2/3)$$
$$k = -\ln(2/3) = 0.405\,465\,108 \simeq 0.41.$$

So the population function is

$$P = 12\,000 - 9000 \exp(-0.41t) \qquad (0 \leq t \leq 10).$$

Note that $P(10)$ according to this formula is approximately 11 850, which is reasonably close to the required value of 12 000.

(b)

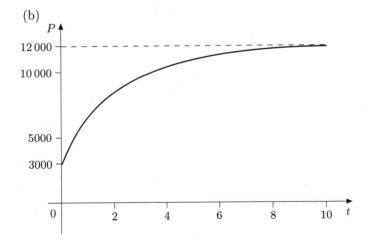

Figure S.9

Solution 3.9

(a) As an appropriate model seems to be a decay-to-a-limit function, start with

$$P = a + b \exp(-kt) \qquad (0 \leq t \leq 12),$$

where P is the rabbit population at t months after the catastrophe.

The given data suggests that $a = 1500$ and $a + b = 5000$. So $b = 5000 - 1500 = 3500$.

The curve must pass through $(1, 3000)$, so

$$3000 = 1500 + 3500 \exp(-k),$$
$$\exp(-k) = \frac{3000 - 1500}{3500} = \frac{3}{7}.$$

Thus $k = -\ln \frac{3}{7} \simeq 0.85$.

So the population function is

$$P = 1500 + 3500 \exp(-0.85t) \qquad (0 \leq t \leq 12).$$

(b)

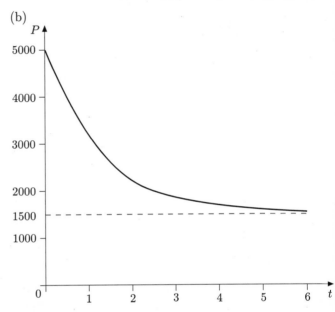

Figure S.10

Solution 3.10

(a) Non-linearity is required by observation 3.

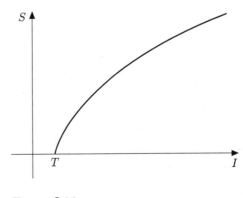

Figure S.11

(b) An exponential-type of growth is not appropriate for a model consistent with these experimental results, since we need a diminishing rate of growth in sensation as the stimulus increases. A growth-to-a-limit type of function is not appropriate since the data, at least over the range of Weber's experiments, do not suggest that there is a limit to the sensation with continuing increase in stimulus; only that the increase in sensation occurs more and more slowly.

Solution 3.11

Starting with

$$y = 3\log\left(\frac{x}{4}\right),$$

divide both sides by 3:

$$y/3 = \log(x/4);$$

raise 10 to the power of each side:

$$10^{y/3} = x/4;$$

multiply both sides by 4 and rearrange, to obtain $x = 4 \times 10^{y/3}$. The associated range is the result of the fact that $x \geq 4$, so $10^{y/3} \geq 1$, so $y/3 \geq 0$ or $y \geq 0$. Thus the relationship is $x = 4 \times 10^{y/3}$ $(y \geq 0)$.

Another way to arrive at the answer is to compare the relationship with the preceding discussion of the Weber–Fechner law. We have y in place of S, x in place of I, 3 in place of A, 4 in place of T. So it is possible to write down

$$x = 4 \times 10^{y/3} \qquad (y \geq 0).$$

Solution 3.12

(a) A sketch of the $\log f$ versus $\log h$ plot that has been described is shown in Figure 3.8. The straight line will have the equation $\log f = \log k + n \log h$. Since the slope is stated to be 0.495, $n = 0.495$. So the function will have the form $f = kh^{0.495}$. The intercept on the $\log f$ axis will correspond to $\log k$. So $\log k = -1$ and $k = 0.1$. Therefore the specific function deduced from this data is

$$f = 0.1h^{0.495} \qquad (1 \leq h \leq 50).$$

(A model for the turbulent flow of liquid from a container predicts $n = 0.5$.)

(b) The intercept on the $\log f$ axis corresponds to $\log h = 0$, or $h = 1$. This is the level in the container at the end of the experiment and is associated with a flow of

$$0.1 \times (1)^{0.495} = 0.11\,s^{-1}.$$

Solution 3.13

(a) Exponential functions are such that the independent variable appears in the exponent (for example, a^x), whereas power law functions have constant exponents (for example, $x^{2.1}$).

(b) Exponential functions lead to log–lin straight lines, whereas power law functions lead to log–log straight lines.

(c) $y = x^{1.2}$ is a power law increase and $y = 1.2^x$ is an exponential increase for $x > 0$. The corresponding straight-line functions are

$$\log y = 1.2 \log x$$
$$\log y = x \log(1.2).$$

Solution 3.14

(a) For $x > 0$, as x increases y decreases in a non-linear way. For $x < 0$, $\dfrac{1}{x^2}$ is positive so y is positive also. As x becomes increasingly negative, y becomes smaller. At $x = 0$, y is undefined so the graph has two parts (see Figure S.12).

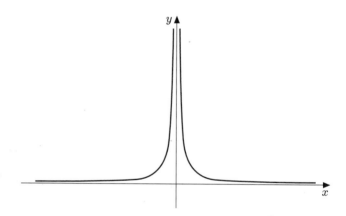

Figure S.12

(b) The addition of the constant, 3, simply shifts the $y = 3x^{-2}$ curve(s) upwards by 3. At $x = 0$, $3x^{-2}$ is still not defined, so y will be undefined as in Figure S.12.

Solution 4.1

(a) The graph of $y = \cos x$ is just the $y = \sin x$ graph shifted to the left, and so the corresponding function has the same amplitude as that of $y = \sin x$, namely 1.

(b) The graph of $y = \sin(2x)$ has the same maximum, minimum and mean values as that of $y = \sin x$ – they are just achieved twice as fast. The graph of $y = 3\sin(2x)$ has three times the difference between (say) the maximum and mean values as does that of $y = \sin(2x)$, so the function $y = 3\sin(2x)$ has amplitude 3.

(c) The '+1' merely shifts the graph in part (b) to the left, so the amplitude is still 3.

(d) The mean value is 3; the *maximum* value $(3 + 4 = 7)$ is achieved when $\sin(2x)$ achieves its *minimum* value; so the amplitude is $7 - 3 = 4$.

(e) Arguing as in (b), the amplitude is $\sqrt{2}$.

Solution 4.2

(a) Since a shift to the left does not affect period, the period of $y = \cos x$ is the same as that of $y = \sin x$, namely 2π.

(b) A complete cycle happens as $2x$ changes from 0 to 2π, so that x changes from 0 to π; thus the period is π.

(c) Shifting the graph in part (b) cannot change the period, so the period is still π.

(d) Shifting the graph upwards and switching 'up' oscillations to 'down' and vice versa cannot change the period, so it is still π.

(e) A complete cycle happens as πx changes from 0 to 2π, so x changes from 0 to 2. Thus the period is 2.

Solution 4.3

(a) Since the period is 2π, an advance in the value of x by 1 takes the function only $\dfrac{1}{2\pi}$ of the way through a cycle, so the frequency is $\dfrac{1}{2\pi}$.

(b) The frequency is $\dfrac{1}{\pi}$.

(c) The frequency is $\dfrac{1}{\pi}$.

(d) The frequency is $\dfrac{1}{\pi}$.

(e) An advance of x by 1 takes this function through half a cycle, so the frequency is $\frac{1}{2}$.

Solution 4.4

The amplitude of the change in water level in the harbour is 3.2 m. The period of the function is given by $2\pi/2.7 = 2.3271$ (corresponding to 2.3271×6 hours $= 13.963$ hours) between high or low tides, and the frequency of the function is $2.7/2\pi = 0.4297$.

Solution 4.5

(a) At the first high tide, $h = 3.2$ and $\sin(0.45t + 2.2168) = 1$,

or $(0.45t + 2.2168) = 5\pi/2$,

$\qquad 0.45t = 5\pi/2 - 2.2168$,

$\qquad t = 12.5271$.

So the first high tide is a little after 12.30 pm.

(b) When the water level is at the mean value,

$$\sin(0.45t + 2.2168) = 0.$$

At the mean level before midnight,

$\qquad 0.45t = -2.2168$

$\qquad t = -4.9262$ (to four decimal places).

So this mean level occurs a little under 5 hours before midnight, i.e. about 7 pm the previous day. The next mean level will occur one half period, or 6.981 hours, later, at approximately 2 am.

Solution 4.7

In the general form $y = a + b\sin(kx + c)$,

the phase $c = 0$, the period $\dfrac{2\pi}{k}$ is 12, so $k = \dfrac{\pi}{6}$;

the amplitude $|b|$ is 2, the mean value a is 5, so

$$L = 5 + 2\sin\left(\frac{\pi}{6}t\right) \qquad (t \geq 0).$$

see note S.P3 P 2

Solution 6.1

An appropriate function should be chosen at Step 2 of the modelling cycle.

Step 5 involves comparing the outcome or prediction of the model with reality. A useful form of 'reality' might be data of some kind. Alternatively, evaluation of the model might involve a check against the original purpose.

Solution 6.2

(a) The rate of decrease in the rate of rainfall over the 20-minute period is specified as steady. The simplest interpretation of this is a *linear* decrease. In general a function of the required form is

$$R = mt + c \qquad (0 \le t \le 20)$$

where m will have to be a negative constant to ensure a decrease.

$R = S$ when $t = 0$, so $c = S$ and the required form is

$$R = mt + S \qquad (0 \le t \le 20).$$

Also we know that $R = 0$ when $t = 20$ (the rain stops after 20 minutes).

$0 = 20m + S$, so $m = -S/20$ and the final result is

$$R = S - \frac{S}{20}t = S\left(1 - \frac{1}{20}t\right) \qquad (0 \le t \le 20).$$

(b) A quadratic decrease is specified. The relevant general form is a parabola

$$Q - b = A(t - a)^2 \qquad (0 \le t \le 4)$$

where a, b and A are constants to be determined from the information given, and we expect A to work out to be negative giving a downward opening parabola. This would correspond to a rate of arrival that changes slowly at first near the vertex of the parabola and then decreases rapidly. Q has its maximum value of 500 at $t = 0$. In this form of the parabola (a, b) are the coordinates of this maximum value. So $a = 0$ and $b = 500$.

The rate of arrival of customers is zero at the end of the sale, so

$$0 - 500 = a(4)^2$$

which means that $A = -31.25$ and the required function is

$$Q = 500 - 31.25t^2 \qquad (0 \le t \le 4).$$

(c) An oscillating function is needed here. A general form is

$$T = a + b\sin(kt + c) \quad (0 \le t \le 24).$$

The maximum value is A and the minimum is B, so the mean, a, must be halfway between the two, $a = B + \dfrac{A - B}{2} = \frac{1}{2}(A + B).$

The amplitude, $b = \frac{1}{2}(A - B).$

The period is 24, so $24 = 2\pi/k$ or $k = \pi/12.$

To ensure that T is minimum at $t = 0$, the phase c should equal $-\pi/2$.

This gives $T = a - b$ at $t = 0$.

So the required function is

$$T = \frac{1}{2}(A + B) + \frac{1}{2}(A - B)\sin\left(\frac{\pi}{12}t - \frac{\pi}{2}\right)$$
$$(0 \le t \le 24).$$

Solutions to Exercises

Solution 1.1

(a) Linear (constant gradient).

(b) The model will only be valid, at some distance after the start of the hill and before the end, as long as the gradient is constant.

Solution 1.2

(a) If h_0 m is the height of water in the barrel at the start of the two-hour period, then a reasonable model based on the information given would be

$$h = h_0 + \frac{0.001}{0.2}t$$
$$= h_0 + 0.005t \quad (0 \le t \le 120).$$

$t = 60 \quad h = 0.005 \times 60 =$

(b) The principal assumptions are: the rainfall is steady, as stated; all the rain drains into the barrel; the cross-sectional area of the barrel is constant. You may also have assumed that the barrel was empty at the start of the timing, in which case $h_0 = 0$.

Solution 1.3

If V litres represents volume and t weeks represents time, then

$$V = 1000 - 120t$$

which is valid only from $t = 0$ until the tank is empty.

$V = 0$ when $0 = 1000 - 120t$
or $t = \dfrac{1000}{120} = 8\frac{1}{3}$, that is, after $8\frac{1}{3}$ weeks.

Solution 2.1

At the time t when the rock hits the roof, the height h is 4, so equation (2.3) gives

$$4 = 35 - 4.9t^2,$$
$$t^2 = \frac{31}{4.9},$$
$$t = \sqrt{\frac{31}{4.9}} = 2.52 \text{ (to two decimal places).}$$

Thus, the rock takes slightly more than 2.5 seconds to hit the roof of the bus.

Solution 2.2

At the highest point of the ball's path:

(a) is not true: the horizontal velocity is constant throughout motion as long as the air resistance is ignored;

(b) is true as long as the air resistance is ignored;

(c) is true;

(d) is not true since the ball is subject to the acceleration due to gravity.

Solution 2.3

(a) If Q cones per hour represents the rate at which customers buy cones, and the maximum rate Q_{max} cones per hour is assumed to occur halfway through the selling day, that is at $t = 4$ where t hours is the time after 10 am, then the appropriate parabolic function is given by

$$Q - Q_{max} = A(t - 4)^2$$

where A is a constant.

(b) The parabola passes through $(0, 0)$ and $(8, 0)$. Using the first of these points,

$$0 - Q_{max} = A(0 - 4)^2$$

or $A = -\dfrac{Q_{max}}{16}$.

Note that the negative value for A is consistent with a downward opening parabola. The model is

$$Q = Q_{max}\left(1 - \tfrac{1}{16}(t - 4)^2\right).$$

(c) The area underneath the parabola represents the total number of cones. So

$$1000 = Q_{max} \int_0^8 \left(1 - \frac{(t-4)^2}{16}\right) dt$$
$$= Q_{max} \int_0^8 \left(1 - \frac{t^2 - 8t + 16}{16}\right) dt$$
$$= Q_{max} \int_0^8 \left(\frac{t}{2} - \frac{t^2}{16}\right) dt$$
$$= Q_{max} \left[\frac{t^2}{4} - \frac{t^3}{48}\right]_0^8$$
$$= Q_{max} \left(16 - \frac{32}{3}\right)$$
$$= 5\tfrac{1}{3} Q_{max}.$$

That is, $Q_{max} = \dfrac{1000 \times 3}{16} = 187.5$, which suggests a maximum rate of about 190 cones per hour.

(d) Assumptions which are made in the above solution are

(i) the maximum rate of sales occurs halfway through the selling day;

(ii) the rate of sales is zero at the time selling starts.

Solution 3.1

(a) $C = 0.5 \exp(-0.04t)$.

(b) When $t = 2.5$,

$$C = 0.5 \exp(-0.1)$$
$$= 0.4524.$$

So the concentration after 2.5 days is predicted to be $0.4524 \, \mathrm{mg \, l^{-1}}$.

Solution 3.2

(a) When $t = 0$, $\exp(-Bt) = 1$, so $Q = 0$.

(b) When t is indefinitely large, $\exp(-Bt)$ approaches zero and Q approaches A.

(c) $\dfrac{dQ}{dt} = AB \exp(-Bt)$.

(d) Growth at an exponentially decreasing rate from 0 at $t = 0$ to a limit of A.

Solution 3.3

Since $\ln y$ is linearly related to x,

$$\ln y = Ax + B$$

for some numbers A, B.

So

$$\tfrac{1}{2} = A + B,$$
$$2 = 3A + B,$$

giving

$$A = \tfrac{3}{4}, \quad B = -\tfrac{1}{4}.$$

Thus

$$\ln y = \tfrac{3}{4}x - \tfrac{1}{4}.$$

Taking the exponential of both sides of this equation and using Rule 2b of Table 3.3 gives

$$y = \exp(\tfrac{3}{4}x - \tfrac{1}{4})$$
$$= \exp(\tfrac{3}{4}x) \times \exp(-\tfrac{1}{4})$$
$$\simeq 0.7788 \exp(\tfrac{3}{4}x).$$

Note that $\exp(\tfrac{3}{4}x)$ may also be written as

$$(e^{3/4})^x \simeq 2.117^x.$$

Solution 3.4

If $y = k \times 2^x$, then by Rules 1, 3 of Table 3.2,

$$\ln y = \ln k + x \ln 2$$
$$\simeq \ln k + 0.69x.$$

The relation is therefore of the form proposed if plotting $\ln y$ against x for the available data pairs produces a straight line whose slope is 0.69. If this occurs, then $\ln k$ is the intercept of the line on the vertical axis.

Solution 4.1

(a) Sinusoidal (through half a cycle).

(b) $\frac{1}{20}$

(c) $t = 0$ and $t = 40$ (since $\sin \pi = 0$).

Solution 4.2

(a) See Figure S.13.

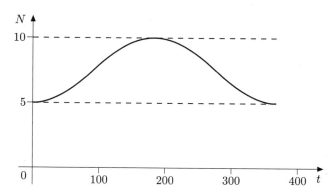

Figure S.13

The function implies a cyclic variation which is appropriate for the purpose.

(b) At $t = 0$, $N = 5$ and $\cos(kt) = 1$, so $5 = a - b$; at $t = \dfrac{\pi}{k}$, $N = 10$ and $\cos(kt) = -1$, so $10 = a + b$.
Hence $a = 7.5$ and $b = 2.5$.
The period is 365 days, so $k = \dfrac{2\pi}{365}$.

(c) When $t = \dfrac{2}{3} \times 365$ or $\dfrac{2}{3} \times \dfrac{2\pi}{k}$,

$$N = 7.5 - 2.5 \cos(\frac{4\pi}{3})$$
$$= 8.75.$$

This predicts 8.75 hours of sunshine.

(d) An assumption is that the day eight months after the middle of winter is an average day and not subject to more than average cloud.

Solution 4.3

(a) The amplitude is $0.001 \, \mathrm{m}$ or $1 \, \mathrm{mm}$. The needle will have travelled through one complete cycle when $30t = 2\pi$. This occurs at a time $t = 2\pi/30 = 0.21$ second.

(b) For the same amplitude, the formula for the needle's position may be expressed as
$$y = 0.001 \sin(kt).$$

The period of the motion is $2\pi/k$ ($= 0.125$ second), so $k = 2\pi/0.125 \simeq 50.3$ and the formula is

$$y = 0.001 \sin(50.3t).$$